with GOD
Nothing Is Impossible:
Walking in the Way

ELAINE A. PHILLIPS

Deep River
BOOKS

With God Nothing Is Impossible: Walking in the Way
Previously published as *With God Nothing Is Impossible: In Step with Women of the Bible*
© 2023, 2014 Elaine A. Phillips

Published by
Deep River Books
Sisters, Oregon
www.deepriverbooks.com

ISBN-13: 9781632696038

Library of Congress Control Number: 2023902144
Printed in the USA

Design by Robin Black, www.InspirioDesign.com

Contents

Foreword

In the years that have followed the first publication of *With God Nothing Is Impossible* (2014), my dear Mama has been ushered into glory. She is indeed of blessed memory (Prov 10:7a), and her gentle wisdom continues to echo in my heart.

Until my retirement, I used this small book with my Old Testament Survey classes. As an encouragement to read faithfully, my students were given the task of journaling, an exercise for which I provided prompts. It was a steady source of joy and encouragement to read their responses. Many of those prompt questions underlie the study and discussion materials now included in this expanded version. I'm thankful to Meredith Nyberg for her contribution toward that section as well.

To God be the glory!

December 2022

Acknowledgments

The seeds for this book were sown in Sri Lanka. One of my former students, Prashan DeVisser, asked if I would accompany a small group of Gordon College students on a short term trip in 2005 to serve in his parents' remarkable church ministry, Kithu Sevena. Part of my task involved speaking to a large gathering of Sri Lankan women, many of whom had recently come to Christ. Stories of God's faithfulness in the lives of biblical women were the obvious starting points. I was grateful to rehearse these narratives—and for my translators who made them vibrate with life. The hospitality of the entire Kithu Sevena community filled my heart with joy and humility.

I am likewise grateful to the friends and colleagues who have kindly consented to read the manuscript and offer their observations and later on, their generous endorsements. I am particularly thankful to the editorial staff at Deep River Books. Prior to publisher Bill Carmichael finding my book proposal lodged on ChristianManuscriptSubmissions.com, I was wryly questioning its title, as several publishers had either rejected or ignored it. Adopted into the DRB family, I have received gracious assistance at every level. Although I hesitate to single out any individual, I would be remiss if I did not offer special thanks to Lee Ann Zanon for her expert editing of each chapter. Any infelicities that remain are entirely my responsibility.

Speaking of family, my dear husband, Perry, has been a constant source of help and encouragement. It is not hyperbole to say he has loved me " . . . just as Christ loved the church and gave himself up for her" (Eph. 5:25). There have been countless times in our forty years of marriage when he has intentionally put his interests second and pushed me to "go for it."

As I write this, my dear ninety-nine-year-old mother, "Mama," is a treasured member of our household. As I have "sat at her feet" over the decades, I have loved and admired her for so many reasons. Her interest in science compelled her to take an undergraduate degree in chemistry, the only woman graduating from the University of Minnesota Institute of Technology in 1942. She worked as a chemist and teacher until my sister and I arrived, at which point she devoted herself to passing along to us her insatiable curiosity, her joy in reading, and her love for science. I remember fondly our first microscope and an ongoing parade of homegrown experiments. Her words, "Boredom is the sign of a small mind," still echo in my head! Once we were in school, she went back to work as a school librarian.

Mama faithfully read to us at bedtime; one of those nightly stories was always a Bible narrative. She was not afraid to ask questions and as we got older, she often expressed them in lively arguments regarding theological issues, among many other topics. She loved nature and taught me how to enjoy lightning, observe columns of ants, and play with garter snakes. Mama was always active, from playing basketball with me after school to cross-country skiing until she was 90. She was a caregiver, first for my grandmother, then my father as he descended slowly and agonizingly into dementia, and finally for numerous friends who needed her "Anderson taxi" for errands. As she has had slowly to relinquish her precious independence, the lesson she is now teaching me (which I pray fervently I will someday learn) comes from her spirit of unfailing gratitude. Even in the face of the shifting contours of her memory, she repeatedly says "thank you." It is with a heart full of my own gratitude that this child "rises up to call her blessed" (Prov. 31:28). This book is dedicated to Mama.

Could This Be True?

With God nothing is impossible." Do you really want to read a book with that title? First of all, it is a double negative, a recipe for confusion. Besides that, what a seemingly impossible declaration . . . one that seldom finds expression in our day-to-day lives. We experience pain, insecurity, frustration, and fear on all sides. The battles against anger, envy, and shame rarely seem to issue forth in victory. While we may easily affirm that nothing is impossible with God, our persistent mindset ironically places the divine Presence far away in the celestial realms, too removed to be involved in our daily impossible situations.

Nevertheless, a foundational theme of the Bible is the perfect and powerful goodness and unfailing love of God. Biblical characters, with all their wounds and scars, were living illustrations that there was a bigger and majestic tapestry and they were part of it. So are we. Nothing was or is outside God's active care for his children.

God's love for those who are weary, have questions and doubts, or face overwhelming challenges is especially compelling when it comes through the narratives of women in the Bible. And what an array of stories we encounter! A remarkable number of these women set out on long and unexpected journeys, not always under the most pleasant circumstances. They were called to venture beyond their own strength and ability. Many wrestled with the task of child-rearing and seemed to have limited success. Each was engaged in tasks that demanded her trust in God and sometimes that God seemed astonishingly inscrutable. We are privileged to learn from those who have gone before us on the journey. Through the pages of Scripture they teach us, and our lives are enriched as we study and pass along life-transforming truth.

We see a pattern for this task in the faithful teaching of Eunice and Lois, Timothy's mother and grandmother. Paul affirmed the immense value of their work when he wrote to Timothy reminding him that the biblical principles he had learned from them had sufficiently prepared him to serve God's church in Ephesus (2 Tim. 1:5, 3:14–17).

One of my earliest memories is of my mother reading to my sister and me each night before we went to bed. The family narrative says that she began that nightly process as soon as she brought us home from the hospital, and although the repertoire of children's books changed, the one standard was always *Hurlbut's Stories of the Bible*. Now it is true that my journey into the faith came about much later and I brought my parents more than their share of grief and gray hairs in the meantime. Nevertheless, the foundation was laid. For that I am ever thankful!

Read the Bible out loud to your children or to anyone who will listen. Talk joyfully about the love of Jesus and the good wisdom of God when you are at home together, when you travel, when you settle down in the evening before bedtime, and when you get up in the morning (Deut. 6:4–7). And may biblical truths weave through the fabric of your conversations so they are not an uncomfortable and artificial overlay!

The women whose steps we trace through these pages are representative of a much greater cloud of witnesses whose lives are part of the remarkable tapestry of God's story. We start with young Mary, uniquely called to a humanly impossible task, and we follow her journey to the foot of the cross. Because her story is writ large in the Gospels, so also here. While we catch only glimpses of others, those fleeting appearances are equally challenging and encouraging. Please join me as we meet these dynamic women and discover the inspiration they offer for our lives today.

Some practical tidbits: because our love for Scripture is enriched when we study in community, I would encourage you to find a small group with whom to read—perhaps even out loud together. Start with the Scriptures noted at the beginning of each chapter and then move into the chapter itself. As you read together, pause when something captures your attention. Each chapter closes with embedded questions and/or further reflections. These in turn connect with more formal study questions at the end of the book. Yes, this takes time; that is true of all things valuable.

Final notes: following the discussion questions, I make suggestions for further reading. All Bible quotations, unless otherwise noted, are from the New International Version.

Timeline: Women of the Bible

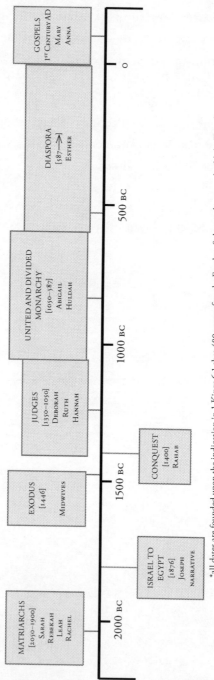

MATRIARCHS
[2050–1900]
SARAH
REBEKAH
LEAH
RACHEL

ISRAEL TO EGYPT
[1876]
JOSEPH NARRATIVE

EXODUS
[1446]
MIDWIVES

CONQUEST
[1400]
RAHAB

JUDGES
[1350–1050]
DEBORAH
RUTH
HANNAH

UNITED AND DIVIDED MONARCHY
[1050–587]
ABIGAIL
HULDAH

DIASPORA
[587→]
ESTHER

GOSPELS
1ST CENTURY AD
MARY
ANNA

2000 BC   1500 BC   1000 BC   500 BC   0

*all dates are founded upon the indication in 1 Kings 6:1 that 480 years after the Exodus, Solomon began to build the Temple
all dates are approximations

ONE

Mary, Mother of God

BIBLICAL TEXTS: MATTHEW 1:18–25, LUKE 1

Who was this woman who was privileged to be the mother of Jesus and the mother of God? Those of us who have grown up with the Christmas story are familiar with Mary as the mother of Jesus. It is mother of *God* that makes us pause. How could we possibly imagine the birth of God? God—who spoke all of creation into existence with his word. God—whose mighty power sustains the vast reaches of the universe. We know that in mysterious ways, God has entered and does enter into our human experience by his merciful choice, but being *born* into it is pretty much over the edge. Not only did God choose to walk among his creatures for a finite amount of time as a fellow human being, teaching and loving and healing; he also humbled himself to experience the birth process, to be weak, helpless, and dirty—like us in every way. Mary was called to be his mother as he took on human flesh.

BORN OF A VIRGIN

And it gets more baffling. The very first thing we are told by Luke is that Mary was a virgin. In fact, the Bible emphasizes this as it introduces her. The angel was sent "to a virgin pledged to be married to a man named Joseph, a descendant of David. The virgin's name was Mary" (Luke 1:27). Whenever the text repeats a characteristic or a name, it is important. *Mary was a virgin.*

This was in contrast to her older relative, Elizabeth. Elizabeth's shame was that she and her husband, Zechariah, were well along in years and had been married a good long time but had no children. In fact, after the angel Gabriel brought the glad tidings to Zechariah that he and Elizabeth would finally have a child and she conceived, she praised God for taking away her disgrace (Luke 1:25). For Elizabeth, having a child removed a longstanding humiliation; for Mary, bearing this Child would bring terrible disgrace at the outset because she was indeed not married. She was a virgin. And she was very young.

We have to ask how God would prepare someone to live with such a burden, and we will return to that. No doubt the months between Mary's visit from Gabriel and her delivery of the Child were filled with tension and anguish. This must have deeply wounded her family in a culture where honor was of utmost importance. Her condition would be the gossip of the town. Who, after all, would believe that kind of a story? Can you imagine your own daughter trying to pull that one on you? Who would help her prepare to give birth, to deal with all the needs of a newborn, to keep her head high as cruel words might circulate?

We also learn that Mary had already been promised in marriage to a man whose name was Joseph. Talk about breaking up a relationship! The gospel of Matthew tells Joseph's side of the story and his concern about the shame of this event. It took another visit from heaven, this time a dream, for Joseph to begin to understand. He then continued his protective relationship with Mary instead of divorcing her quietly (Matt. 1:19). The commitment of betrothal for that culture was sufficiently binding that breaking off the "engagement" would be the equivalent of divorce. Despite Joseph's honorable behavior, in a small town where most folks were just about as skeptical and critical as our own neighbors, they would likely live their lives on the margins of "proper society" for a good long while.

It is the bitter experience of many dear and vulnerable young women that, once their reputation has been tarnished, the stigma clings. Nevertheless, we discover in Mary a young woman who was entirely submissive to the will of her God, even though it meant heart-wrenching doses of humiliation. In her lifetime, she knew little of the honor that later generations of Christians would grant to her.

THE ANGEL'S WORDS TO MARY

Gabriel greeted Mary as "you who are highly favored," declaring that the Lord was with her (Luke 1:28). For some reason, this troubled her greatly. To be sure, when angels had appeared to people in Old Testament narratives their presence was terrifying. So much for chubby-faced Valentine's Day cherubs! In fact, in his next breath, the angel told her not to be afraid. Nevertheless, Luke says the angel's *words* disturbed Mary. What did it mean that she was highly favored and the Lord was with her? How could words have such power? But those were only the start! The angel went on to promise that this Child, her Son, would be the promised deliverer. It may be an indication of Mary's deep humility that words such as these, words that exalted her person and identity, brought a sense of profound distress to her heart.

Mary's story unfolds against the rich tapestry of Old Testament narratives and promises and the painful realities for first-century Jews in Palestine. The Jewish people were under the harsh rule of Roman occupation and they suffered from internal strife as well. They might well have wondered if God had forgotten his promises to deliver them from all manner of injustice and oppression. And here the angel was telling Mary that *she* would have a son named Jesus, whose name means "the Lord saves." He would be "Son of the Most High" and "Son of David." All of these exalted titles meant one thing. *Her* son would be the Anointed Savior.

Mary likely would have been familiar with the words of Isaiah that echoed throughout the angel's declaration: "For to us a child is born, to us a son is given, and the government will be on his shoulders. And he will be called Wonderful Counselor, Mighty God, Everlasting Father, Prince of Peace. Of the increase of his government and peace there will be no end. He will reign on David's throne and over his kingdom, establishing and upholding it with justice and righteousness from that time on and forever. The zeal of the Lord Almighty will accomplish this" (Is. 9:6-7).

NOT AFRAID TO ASK QUESTIONS

Mary declared her innocence. "How will this be, since I am a virgin?" (Luke 1:34). It was humanly impossible without the involvement of Joseph—and that, of course, was the point! This was the most astonishing of miracles by which *God* would take on human flesh and blood. But that flesh and blood would be pure; that is the importance of the virgin birth. The angel gave a few more details, none of which we can begin really to comprehend. "The Holy Spirit will come upon you, and the power of the Most High will overshadow you . . ." (Luke 1:35). There are echoes here of creation's story when the Holy Spirit hovered over the waters (Gen 1:2). God's eternity was invading human space and time in a most holy and powerful demonstration. His infinity was about to be captured in Mary's womb. How must she have felt beginning this pregnancy, her first? What an unfathomable combination! On the one hand, normal symptoms; on the other, the knowledge that the new life developing within her was the result of God's power infusing her very being! None of this could be easily spoken. No wonder that later Luke tells us Mary treasured and pondered all these things in her heart (Luke 2:19).

Mary's question may have had further layers. "How can this be . . . ?" How could God do this to her? To be sure, purity was preserved in one sense, but *Mary's* purity would be questioned; she would be presumed to be an utter disgrace. Isn't it interesting that Mary would share the reversals and the humiliations that were the fabric of Jesus's life? His opponents always suspected the worst about him; it was likely the case with Mary as well.

The angel ended his announcement by saying "For nothing is impossible with God" (Luke 1:37). After hearing the angel's assurance, Mary's simple and deep faith took over. "I am the Lord's servant," Mary answered. "May it be to me as you have said" (Luke 1:38). No further questions; no expressed fears; no worries about destructive rumors and gossip. "May it be to me as you have said." In essence Mary declared, "I accept God's will for the rest of my life." Words are insufficient to express the awe that her faithfulness engenders.

What anguish and uncertainty do we have in our lives that seem too difficult for us to bear? What causes us unrest and fear? Can we say along with Mary, "May it be to me as God has ordained"? These words, by the way, are not the end of what she said. We will discover more in the next chapter. But at this point in her life, she *believed* God and declared herself to be the Lord's servant.

TWO

Mary's Trust in God's Truth

MARY'S VISIT TO ELIZABETH

The reality of small-town gossip and suspicion may have been what sent Mary from Nazareth in Galilee to visit Elizabeth in Judea, near Jerusalem. This would have been a rugged three or four day journey for someone in her condition. It was difficult, dangerous, and unthinkable for a woman to travel on her own, but who would have accompanied her? Perhaps a reluctant relative; we do not know.

When Elizabeth, six months pregnant with John the Baptist, saw Mary, the Holy Spirit filled her heart with knowledge of the truth. By his Spirit, God revealed to these two women that Mary *would be the mother of the Lord* (Luke 1:43). And then Elizabeth affirmed Mary's own faith: "Blessed is she who has believed that what the Lord has said to her will be accomplished!" (Luke 1:45). Here were two women, one past the age of bearing children now with child, and the other so young, it hardly seemed possible that she would be ready for this responsibility. Together they were the Lord's servants. Both were embarking on the sobering journey of motherhood for the first time.

MARY'S SONG: BASED ON GOD'S PROMISES

When Mary heard Elizabeth's blessing, her own heart was filled, and she burst forth in a song that demonstrated how very well she knew the Scriptures. As she sang the praise and blessings of God, echoes of the Psalms and of the song of Hannah, the mother of Samuel, were all woven together. She did not wail about her own fears and apprehensions. Instead, deeply aware of the honor of her task, she gave all praise to the Lord, just as the authors of the Psalms did repeatedly and just as Samuel's mother did when God promised her the long-awaited son.

> "My soul magnifies the Lord,
> and my spirit rejoices in God my Savior,
> for he has looked on the humble estate of his servant.
> For behold, from now on all generations will call me blessed;
> for he who is mighty has done great things for me,
> and holy is his name.
> And his mercy is for those who fear him
> from generation to generation.
> He has shown strength with his arm;
> he has scattered the proud in the thoughts of their hearts;
> he has brought down the mighty from their thrones
> and exalted those of humble estate;
> he has filled the hungry with good things,
> and the rich he has sent away empty.
> He has helped his servant Israel,
> in remembrance of his mercy,
> as he spoke to our fathers,
> to Abraham and to his offspring forever." (Luke 1:46–55, ESV)

Mary's song focused on the truths that would be a major part of Jesus' teaching ministry. He came to turn our selfish expectations up-side-down. The first would be last and the last first. Those who were poor were blessed; the humble would inherit the earth. Mary's song affirmed God's good and tender mercy to those who were downtrodden. He would bring down the rich and lift up the humble. Mary was clearly one of those persons at the bottom of the social ladder. But she *knew* that this Son of hers would play a major part in extending the tender and compassionate love of God to people. These were God's truths, from God's Word, and Mary knew how to think of her life and circumstances in light of that reality, even though her situation was frightening and filled with uncertainty.

How consistently do we process our circumstances through the truth of Scripture? Can we say, "My soul magnifies the Lord and my spirit *rejoices* in God," when our most intimate human relationships are foundering? When shame seems to be the dominant feature of our existence? When fears lurk around every emotional corner? The only way Mary could possibly hold fast to her faith was by standing on the firm foundation of truth she had planted deep in her heart, so that when she sang, she sang Scripture. The words of the classic hymn, "How Firm a Foundation," by John Rippon, echo her example:

> *How firm a foundation, ye saints of the Lord,*
> *Is laid for your faith in His excellent word!*
> *What more can He say than to you He hath said,*
> *To you who for refuge to Jesus have fled?*

ELIZABETH BORE JOHN THE BAPTIST

At the end of Mary's three month stay in Judea, Elizabeth's son would have been born; perhaps Mary saw this nephew of hers before she left for home in Nazareth. The shame of Elizabeth's barrenness was ended; she had a long-awaited son and his name would be John.

There is, however, a sad undertone in this story. Given their advanced ages at the birth of John, Elizabeth and Zechariah may not have lived long enough to see him into adulthood. From Luke 1:80, we learn that John grew up in the wilderness. That is not where the family had lived, since they were from the hill country in Judea, and the wilderness was an unlikely place to rear a child. It was a stark and barren wasteland, but home to small communities who loved God and God's covenant, were waiting for His return, and called themselves "sons of Zadok"—priests. Because both Elizabeth and Zechariah were of priestly descent, they may have arranged for John's continued care within a "safe" environment. We can only wonder how his aging mother felt, especially if he was still quite young when she and Zechariah died.

MARY AND JOSEPH JOURNEY TO BETHLEHEM

Meanwhile, as Mary neared the end of her pregnancy under Joseph's care, the Roman government issued a decree that everyone had to register for purposes of a taxation census (Luke 2:1). To accomplish this, they had to return to their ancestral homes. Joseph was from the tribe of Judah and a descendant of David. That meant he and Mary had to travel from Nazareth to Bethlehem, the home town of David. While this was an order coming from the Roman occupying force, it was more importantly God's way of fulfilling a long-standing and very significant prophecy. Seven hundred years before this, Micah had prophesied that the long-expected ruler would come from Bethlehem. "But you, Bethlehem Ephrathah, though you are small among the clans of Judah, out of you will come for me one who will be ruler over Israel, whose origins are from of old, from ancient times" (Mic. 5:2). In God's perfect timing, Mary and Joseph set out for Bethlehem for the birth of her child.

It was a difficult journey of about seventy-five or eighty miles, and the last part would have meant a constant uphill climb into the mountains of Judea, not easy under any circumstances. And so we can imagine Mary treading on toward the fulfillment of her pregnancy, and the prophecy as well.

THE BIRTH OF JESUS

We have no idea how long it was after they arrived that Mary went into labor, but we know Bethlehem was crowded with people who had returned to register there. In fact, because the royal line of David was so significant, an even larger number of people may have been returning to Bethlehem than to other cities; it was an honor to claim that Davidic heritage. No doubt Joseph's lineage assured the couple of honorable treatment as much as was possible in the crowded conditions. It is not likely they were shunted into a remote cattle shed, even though the guest rooms in all the homes were already occupied. First-century village homes were small, but often had a semi-separate guest room, sometimes approached by a short set of steps. The rest of the home included under its roof the animals' nighttime shelter, complete with feeding troughs. It could be that Mary and Joseph found themselves staying in the lower room of a house near the warmth of the animals. Many homes incorporated natural caves. Mary and Joseph may have spent some days, perhaps even longer, in such an arrangement.

How Mary's life had been overturned again and again! She was to be the mother of the Lord God, and what followed? A most peculiar pregnancy, a forced journey with Joseph to Bethlehem, and giving birth to the Son of God, Savior, in grimy conditions. How that must have tested her faith in the God whose praises she had sung! We're not told what she thought or how she felt. We might guess that the *power* of Gabriel's message and her *knowledge* of its truth carried her through the wrenching pain and uncertainty. Having given birth, she wrapped the baby and put him in a nearby feeding trough, what we commonly call the manger.

THE SHEPHERD'S VISIT

At this point in the story, we read of the angel's glorious announcement to the shepherds. "Today in the town of David a Savior has been born to you; he is Christ [the Messiah], the Lord. This will be a sign to you: You will find a baby wrapped in strips of cloth and lying in a manger" (Luke 2:11-12). Shepherds were a rough lot; they lived in the fields with their sheep and were not among the most respected people. But here's the beauty of this part of the story. When the shepherds hurried into Bethlehem and found the baby Jesus, they discovered that this Savior was *for them*. He was not born into riches, cloistered away from the unruly swirl of life. He was one of them!

Imagine Mary's perspective at this point. There she was, exhausted after delivering her baby. In burst a crowd of rugged shepherds, trying to explain what they had just seen and heard out in the field, and wanting to see the child. It's the stuff of fiction! But Mary believed, and the shepherds believed, and they went out and told everyone in sight. We, too, are called as believing witnesses of God's love.

FURTHER REFLECTIONS

Mary's story covers a wide range of wrenching emotions. At the start, she came face-to-face with humiliation and shame, probably among the most painful emotions to endure because they happen in public and are so difficult to overcome. Then there was joy! And, doubtless everything in between.

We might ask ourselves how we have worked through seemingly impossible circumstances, those brimming with uncertainty and anguish. Is it possible, imploring God for the presence of His Holy Spirit, to respond with humility and grace, saying, "May it be to me as God has ordained"?

Several years ago, I studied the life of Fanny Crosby, one of America's foremost hymn writers from the nineteenth century. By all accounts, she was a remarkable woman, having written more than 8,000 hymns. Even more compelling, however, is the fact that she was blind from the age of six weeks. That could be grounds for wallowing in despair all her life. Nevertheless, she could "see" in ways that seem somehow to elude most of us, and among the things she saw were the transforming beauty of God's grace for sinners and the firm hope God's people have in Jesus. Before she was ten years old, she had memorized the first four books of the Old Testament, and also the four Gospels. Among Fanny Crosby's most memorable hymn texts are: "To God Be the Glory, great things He has done; so loved He the world that He gave us His Son"; and "Blessed Assurance, Jesus is Mine; oh what a foretaste of glory divine." What a marvelous legacy of both knowing and speaking the word of God faithfully!

Let me also mention Frances Ridley Havergal. By the age of twenty-two, she knew by heart the entire New Testament, the Psalms, and Isaiah, and was beginning to memorize the Minor Prophets! The biblical truths that shaped her deep commitment to Jesus shine forth in some of her most well-known lyrics: "Take my life and let it be consecrated, Lord, to Thee"; and "Like a river glorious is God's perfect peace."

It is no wonder these women wrote poetry with such rich theology. Clearly, they invested countless hours in searching and memorizing the Scriptures. You may be thinking, "Get a life!" Actually, that is precisely what they were doing—with much more lasting impact than some of the things we think of as "real living." We have much to learn from their examples.

What if we start by memorizing one entire Psalm? Psalms 103 and 121 are good choices, or perhaps you have other favorites. As we see the power of God's truth to strengthen our trust and transform our lives, let us continue to relish this wonderful gift and soak up as much as we possibly can. It is not in vain. God will use those Scriptures that we have memorized to bless others. Remember the legacies of Fanny Crosby and Frances Havergal—and Mary.

THREE

Mothering God in His Early Years

BIBLICAL TEXTS: MATTHEW 2; LUKE 2:21–52

Think of Mary's life for the next thirty years or so. We've only a few glimpses of it in the Bible, but each one is heartbreaking from a mother's perspective. Whenever there was joy at the work her Son was called to do, there was a current of impending anguish. It commenced immediately as this new family set out to keep the Jewish law related to purification after childbirth and dedication to the Lord (Lev. 12).

SIMEON'S MESSAGE: "A SWORD WILL PIERCE YOUR OWN SOUL"

In obedience to God's commands, Mary and Joseph took Jesus to the temple in Jerusalem to present him to the Lord. We know they were poor by the kind of sacrifice they brought for the dedication. It was a pair of pigeons, designated for the most destitute who came as pilgrims to the temple. There Mary and Joseph met a righteous and good man named Simeon. He was filled with the Holy Spirit, and he took Jesus in his arms and said, " . . . my eyes have seen your salvation, which you have prepared in the sight of all people, a light for revelation to the Gentiles, and for glory to your people Israel" (Luke 2:30–32).

A warm surge of pride must have flooded Mary's heart at those words. The promises—light for the Gentiles and glory for Israel—likely reminded her of the prophet Isaiah. And then Simeon said to her, "This child is destined to cause the falling and rising of many in Israel, and to be a sign that will be spoken against, so that the thoughts of many hearts will be revealed. And a sword will pierce your own soul too" (Luke 2:34-35). Joy turned to apprehension and perhaps stunned disbelief. Some thirty years later, Mary would have the unbearable sorrow of helplessly watching her beloved Son be crucified as a criminal. By the way, Simeon's message was confirmed by the prophetic voice of Anna, a widow who made the temple her home—worshiping, fasting, and praying day and night. She spoke of *this* Child to all who were honestly seeking the redemption of Jerusalem (Luke 2:36–38).

We might ask what that meant to Mary. The fact that she and Joseph went to Jerusalem to fulfill the requirements of the Torah meant that she would know "redemption" as a procedure for buying back firstborn sons (Exod. 13), land, and property (note the book of Ruth). She would know that God had redeemed his people from bondage in Egypt; that was their national epic story, and its meaning of freedom infused the prophetic words for centuries to come. She would know that God himself is called Redeemer innumerable times in the Old Testament. ". . . you will know that I, the LORD, am your Savior, your Redeemer, the Mighty One of Jacob" (Isa. 60:16). No doubt she also shared the hopes of her fellow first-century Jews for freedom from Roman oppression. What a weight of glory on the shoulders of her tiny Son! And how would she handle it?

THE VISIT OF THE WISE MEN

When the family returned from Jerusalem to Bethlehem, they seem to have spent some time there, maybe so much as two years. Perhaps they thought of settling down. It would be a more comfortable place than Nazareth; no cruel gossip would follow their every step. But other forces were moving, far beyond their control. Mary and Joseph would soon flee the rage and paranoia of Herod the Great.

Herod was not a Jew but an Idumean, an ethnic group forcibly converted to Judaism in the century before Christ. He was, however, king of the Jews, having officially been given that position by the Senate in Rome. His reign was not easily established; he took the kingdom bit by bit through brutal warfare. At this time, he was near the end of his life, had endured plots against him, and had murdered several of his sons and his favorite wife because of his deep paranoia. When a small group of wise men from the east appeared in Jerusalem, asking where they might find the one who was "*born* King of the Jews" (Matt. 2:2), Herod's terror of losing his kingdom intensified even more.

The wise men no doubt thought that the court was as good as any place to start looking, but they seem to have made a wider impression. Matthew's Gospel tells us that all of Jerusalem was disturbed along with Herod (Matt. 2:3). "*Born* king." This was certainly troubling and unwelcome news in certain quarters. In Israel's history, there were times when very young boys had been established as king in the face of evil rulers. The names Joash and Josiah might have rung in the mind of Herod—if he was sufficiently aware of the heritage to recognize them. Was this a potential coup by Jewish groups who hated his rule?

Herod was smart enough to know that if anyone had the answer to the wise men's question, it would be those who studied the books of the Prophets. And so he called the chief priests and teachers of the law, and they quoted Micah 5:2 straight away—the answer was Bethlehem. Of course, the city of David. In Herod's mind, this could be a real threat to his own dynastic hopes. Nearing the end of his life, he still had several sons he had not murdered. *They* were to be kings, not an unknown baby in Bethlehem whose parents would claim supposed Davidic connections. He sent the wise men to Bethlehem, urging them to come back and report their findings. His intent was to arrange for this child's death. As it turned out, there would instead be the slaughter of innocent children.

Mary and Joseph were at home when the wise men arrived. Sometimes these men are called magi; sometimes kings. They were noble foreigners and there they were, kneeling in front of Jesus, who was with Mary. If Mary had any doubts as to whether the prophecy of the angel was true, here was dramatic confirmation. Kings bowed before her baby Jesus and worshiped him.

In addition, they gave him gold, incense, and myrrh, all very costly. Mary would know some of the meaning of this. Gold was for a king. Incense was burned by priests offering sacrifices in the temple. The sight of myrrh might have made her shudder. It was used to prepare bodies for burial. We have no record of what the wise men said to Mary, or her responses. No doubt the magi found something far different from what they expected. Perhaps they were stunned into silence. What would happen to their expensive gifts in the care of this simple and poor family? And Mary—what would she say? "Thank you; thank you for gifts so extremely valuable; thank you for entrusting them to us. We'll keep them for him; we certainly will. Thank you for making this long journey to honor my Son. Will you stay the night? We have little to offer, but do stay before you set out again."

WARNINGS IN DREAMS

Wherever the wise men slept that night, two very important dreams were dreamt. The wise men were warned in a dream not to go back to Herod. Joseph was instructed by an angel to get up and flee to Egypt with Mary and Jesus. That very night, Mary's life went from temporary stability, security, and calm to upheaval. She hastily packed their few belongings (with the treasures of the kings securely hidden among them) in order to escape the fury of Herod. When he realized he had been outsmarted, Herod ordered the murder of all baby boys in Bethlehem under the age of two. Did Mary and Joseph hear of this carnage? No doubt. How did Mary respond, knowing that her baby was safe, but other mothers were wailing in terror as Herod's brutal forces rampaged through the night streets?

THE JOURNEY TO EGYPT

Travel to Egypt was difficult and long, even more than coming from Nazareth to Bethlehem. It meant crossing the barren expanse of northern Sinai and entering a foreign land. The only comfort was that there was already a very large community of Jews in Egypt. Mary and Joseph would be able to settle among some of their own people; there would be solace in that. And so they fled, just ahead of Herod's furious slaughter of the baby boys in Bethlehem. Matthew quotes Jeremiah, ". . . Rachel weeping for her children . . ." (Matt. 2:18), knowing that his reading audience would be able to finish the passage: "Rachel weeping for her children and refusing to be comforted, *because her children are no more*" (Jer. 31:15). On an exponentially larger scale, we think of the deaths of millions of Jewish children in the Holocaust and are plunged into horror at the visceral evil that propagates crimes of such magnitude.

Their time in Egypt was not very long. Mary and Joseph learned of Herod's death and wanted to return home, perhaps back to Bethlehem instead of Nazareth. That made sense because it fit the prophecy. Their boy, after all, was the Son of David. There would be fewer wagging tongues there, it would be closer to Jerusalem, and it may have seemed certain to them that this was where Jesus should grow up. Nevertheless, they did return to Nazareth in Galilee. Joseph was again warned in a dream that corresponded to his waking fears; Herod's son Archelaus was ruling in Judea and his presence was just as threatening as his father's.

GROWING UP IN NAZARETH

The Gospels are essentially silent about Jesus' boyhood. We can only imagine life in Nazareth for the growing family. Jesus eventually came to have both brothers and sisters (Matt. 13:55-56). We wonder if Mary told them or anyone else anything of what she knew about him. How could she? Who in her circle of family and neighbors would ever understand the angel's message, the words spoken at the temple, or the gifts of the wise men? Even more subtly, Mary may have struggled with occasional comments about her firstborn son. Luke says Mary pondered these things in her heart. It is a theme to which we repeatedly return. She was a remarkable woman, keeping silent when it was important to do so.

Mary and Joseph undoubtedly made mistakes as young parents. It is a profound challenge to raise *any* child, but what about the *perfect* child, surrounded by those of sinful human stock? How could Mary avoid comparing her children? And yet how fatal that is! How did Mary and Joseph handle their own errors and how would Jesus have responded? In the book of Hebrews, we are told that Jesus learned obedience through suffering (Heb. 5:8). A part of that process might have been his experience of being obedient to imperfect parents. From Mary's side, we can only imagine how her lapses as the mother of *this* child must have grieved her. We're only given one brief look at her experience in that realm.

JESUS' VISIT TO THE TEMPLE: HIS FATHER'S HOUSE

As the son of God-fearing parents, Jesus would have gone regularly to synagogue where he studied Torah (the laws and instructions in the Books of Moses) and engaged in activities that might be mirrored in churches today—prayer, singing, reading the Scriptures. The family undoubtedly also went faithfully to Jerusalem for the three annual festivals, just as the law commanded. None of this, however, prepared Jesus' parents for the experience at the Jerusalem temple when he was 12.

They had gone for Passover as usual. Huge crowds attended this celebration, arriving in Jerusalem from all over the country and beyond. Those who came from a distance had to get there at least four days early in order to purchase the lamb and be certain it was without blemish (Exod. 12:3–6). We can imagine the press of the crowds, bleating lambs, shrill voices, hawkers with food to sell, haggling over prices, and

exchanges among those who spoke only minimal Hebrew. It was probably not very different from Jerusalem today where more than 130 languages are spoken, and crowds of pilgrims churn through the narrow
streets of the Old City.

When the Israelites ate the Passover together in their families, they
were celebrating God's great miracle of deliverance from Egypt hun-
dreds of years before. This was their national narrative and the pilgrim
throng, including Mary, Joseph, and their family, would have held
every aspect of that tradition dear to their hearts. The centerpiece of
the Passover ritual was daubing the blood of the lamb over the doors
and on the doorposts of the Israelites' homes in Egypt. It protected
God's people from His burning anger against the false gods of the
Egyptians. In the same way, the blood of Jesus protects us from God's
great wrath against the false gods that have invaded our lives, made
us greedy and fearful, and demanded our allegiance. When Jesus was
crucified, he was that Passover Lamb, freeing us from the bondage of
all of our twisted habits (1 Cor. 5:6–8).

After celebrating Passover, Mary and Joseph stayed an additional
seven days for the feast of Unleavened Bread. Getting rid of leaven or
yeast was originally intended to remind the people of Israel that they
had left Egypt in haste on that first Passover, before their bread was
able to rise. Over the years, however, it developed a deeper meaning.
Leaven came to symbolize evil. Getting rid of leaven for those seven
days and eating only unleavened bread (matzah) was a reminder to
the Jews that they were to be God's pure people, free from sin.

When the festival was over, the joyful crowds began the journey
home. It was springtime and the land would have been renewed from
the winter rains. There were large extended caravans of people—friends,
relatives, neighbors—rejoicing at the pleasure of another good holiday.
They journeyed for a day before Mary and Joseph discovered Jesus
was not anywhere among their relatives and friends. A lost child is
horrifying. Most of us have had the experience of having our little one

wandering and slipping out of sight amongst the knees of the usual assortment of adults. But losing *this* Child was dreadful beyond words. Not knowing what else to do, Mary and Joseph turned around, retracing their steps to Jerusalem. What a disappointment it was to leave the throng of pilgrims! And imagine their fear, not only for Jesus, but because they had to travel alone up to Jerusalem. The roads were not always safe. As a matter of fact, Jesus would later tell a parable about a man beaten by robbers on that very same road (Luke 10:25–37).

When they arrived in Jerusalem, they searched for three days. Perhaps they looked in places they had stayed, perhaps through all the streets now empty of Passover pilgrims. They may not have thought right away of going to the temple. After all, what would Jesus be doing there? He was too young to find his way through its complex rooms and corridors. When they did venture to the temple, however, there he was with the teachers of the Law, the greatest minds in Judaism.

The Bible says Jesus was listening and asking questions (Luke 2:46). Asking questions was (and is) a significant part of Jewish learning and discussion. It means he was accepted as an active participant in the conversation. This interaction far exceeded his synagogue instruction, and his parents were astonished. Nevertheless, Mary did scold him for having caused them such great anxiety. Jesus' answer must have both puzzled her and deeply cut to her heart, "Didn't you know I had to be in My Father's house?" (Luke 2:49) And that is all he said.

Luke tells us that afterward, Jesus returned to Nazareth with Mary and Joseph and was obedient. It seems that his divine identity was concealed and he grew up as a normal child. Think of the self-sacrifice and complete humiliation this involved. He became not only human, but a human child subject to all the trials of growing up in a family. Squabbles, jealousies, accidents, and frustration were part of the household fare, right along with love and joy.

Immediately after the simple but astounding note about Jesus' obedience to his parents, the Bible again says, "Mary treasured all these things in her heart . . ." (Luke 2:51). The first time we read that phrase, in Luke 2:19, Mary had just experienced childbirth and had entertained rough and tumble shepherds who couldn't stop talking about the angelic hosts and their good news of the Savior. Small wonder that she treasured each of those words and actions, and reflected long about the glorious meaning of all of it all. How often we revisit and savor precious moments such as those!

FURTHER REFLECTIONS

But, what about now? No doubt Mary's memory "treasury" had grown more complex. There would have been incidents that demonstrated her own failure to understand her Son. Perhaps she wrestled with an overwhelming sense of inadequacy as she engaged in daily parenting tasks for this child and his siblings. How was she to put all this together? Given her deep trust in her God, we can be assured that part of her "treasuring" was praying, seeking God's guidance, pleading for forgiveness, and committing herself to learning from her mistakes. One thing was for certain; she could be assured of Jesus' love for her; it was deeply intertwined with his obedience at every turn.

So also we, like Mary, can be absolutely confident of Jesus' love. For us he was "obedient to death, even death on a cross!" (Phil. 2:8). And as we rest in Jesus, we pray earnestly for deeper insight and closer communion with God as we arrange and polish the gems in our memory treasuries.

FOUR

Dashed Expectations

BIBLICAL TEXTS: JOHN 2:1–12; LUKE 4:14–30;
MATTHEW 12:46–50; JOHN 19:26-27; MATTHEW 28:1–7

Think about the trouble you occasionally have understanding your daughter or son, especially in those challenging adolescent years. Does it feel as if you speak different languages when you try to talk about decisions and choices? I recall my mother often saying in retrospect that she just wished I would talk instead of maintaining a stony, sullen silence. Yet even when we are blessed to have ongoing conversations in our families, our words often work at cross purposes! "Didn't you hear me say . . .?" "But that's not what you said." "I did say it; you just weren't paying attention."

Now take those exchanges and think how the challenges escalate when family members' words and actions become more public and reflect on us, often in ways that cause a pink flush to creep up our necks. Imagine Mary as she was both unreservedly proud of Jesus and his growing reputation and scandalized at the odd developments that transpired in certain events. And imagine her injured motherly love at some of what he said, especially in public.

THE WEDDING FEAST AT CANA

When Jesus was about thirty, his quiet life in Nazareth suddenly changed. He was baptized by his cousin John in the Jordan River, an event that inaugurated his public ministry. Jesus heard the voice of the Father affirming that this was his beloved Son, and he saw the presence of God's Spirit descending as a dove. These were visible and audible demonstrations of His authority to be God's anointed Servant. Jesus began to gather followers, and he left the family business to his brothers. One of his first eyebrow-raising actions occurred at a wedding celebration in a small town near Nazareth.

No doubt Mary knew the family; she could well have had a part in the wedding reception since she was aware right away of the humiliating prospect of running out of wine. Perhaps the larger number of guests created by the arrival of Jesus and his disciples drained the wine vessels a bit earlier than the hosts had expected. Mary knew Jesus could do something about it. She also thought that he *should*, and she made that quite clear, going ahead and ordering the servants to do whatever Jesus said. In turn, Jesus' seemingly sharp response to her made it sound as if he would not do anything, but he did. He turned ordinary water, about 120 gallons (or about 240 liters) of it, into fine wine. This was more than enough to rescue the groom from an embarrassing scene; the leftovers also gave the newly married couple a splendid wedding present, setting them up financially for months, even years. And Mary had prompted Jesus to do this.

How pleased she must have been with *her* Son! What a wonderful beginning! And with so much more to come! But her expectations would be severely challenged. There were *other* things God would do.

PREACHING IN THE SYNAGOGUE IN NAZARETH

Mary may have been present the first day Jesus preached in the synagogue in Nazareth. Everyone was pleased, especially as he read from the prophet Isaiah, "The Spirit of the LORD is on me, because He has anointed me to preach good news to the poor. He has sent me to proclaim freedom for the prisoners and recovery of sight for the blind, to release the oppressed, to proclaim the year of the LORD's favor" (Isa. 61:1-2, as quoted in Luke 4:18-19). The people eagerly waited for his sermon on the text. He sat down and said, "Today this Scripture is fulfilled in your hearing."

The promises that Jesus read had to do with the coming of the Deliverer, the Messiah, the Anointed One. He claimed to be that Person—how exhilarating! These were promises Mary had treasured for decades, and now Jesus was publicly claiming them. But in short order he intentionally angered the whole synagogue congregation. Mary's face might have turned red from embarrassment as her son declared that "no prophet is accepted in his hometown," leaving no doubt that he was challenging them. He taunted them with reminders that God had sent their signature prophets, Elijah and Elisha, not to Israel but to foreigners. They did not have exclusive rights to the mercies of God after all.

Mary must have wished in her heart that he would soften his tone, but he did not. Enraged and insulted, the people hauled him to a high cliff near the town to push him over to a certain death. Even though he walked away unharmed, consider Mary's awkward position of unswerving loyalty to her Son mingled with shame and regret that he was so outspoken. Yet again, Mary was possibly the subject of cruel gossip in Nazareth. It was not long after this that Jesus moved to Capernaum with his mother and brothers (John 2:12).

"HERE ARE MY MOTHER AND MY BROTHERS"

Mary made one more appearance during the days of Jesus' public ministry. On this occasion, too, we wonder how she dealt with the painful events that had accompanied her ever since the day Gabriel announced she would have this Child. Matthew tells us that while Jesus was preaching, his mother and brothers arrived, waiting to speak to him (Matt. 12:46). Jesus' message had hardly been warm and soothing; he issued a stern warning to those who *saw* his miracles and still hardened their hearts. We don't know why his mother and brothers came. Perhaps they were curious about the crowds that gathered around him.

On the other hand, perhaps they were worried about the kinds of things he was doing and saying. Maybe they had come to take him home and off the public scene. After all, his trouble would be family trouble and the family did not need any more embarrassment. Nevertheless, when Jesus was told of their presence, he seemed to have disregarded the family ties. Instead, he pointed to his followers and called *them* family—mother and brothers. How that must have been a sword through Mary's soul—as Simeon had forewarned—and there would be more! What was she pondering now? It would have been easy for her to nurse that painful wound. But this was the Mary who sang her way through the days of her miraculous and scandalous pregnancy. Older, yes. Careworn, no doubt, especially since it seems that Joseph had died at some point and she was on her own with this unusual family. Nevertheless, the web of Scripture woven in her heart was stronger than ever.

ON THE ROAD TO THE CROSS

This Son of hers continued to bring joy and hope to the common folks but angered the Pharisees and temple leadership. His miracles could not be denied, but some attributed them to the power of Satan. Jesus' home town of Capernaum—where Mary had come to live—had seen his mighty works. Even so, there was a strong current of unbelief. What could Mary do as she continued to hear the jibes and accusations, both in Capernaum and beyond, as Jesus set His face to go to Jerusalem? She likely turned and returned to the only comfort she knew would not fail her, the Psalms of her people.

Mary was in Jerusalem at Passover and she was at the foot of the cross when her Son was tortured and mocked. She was there to hear her firstborn Son, who was responsible for her welfare after the death of Joseph, give her into the care of his Beloved Disciple John. She heard him say, "Father forgive them; they do not know what they are doing," when they were nailing him naked and humiliated to the cross (Luke 23:34). She heard him cry out of the depths "My God, My God, why have you forsaken me?" as the Eternal Father in heaven poured out his judgment against sin onto *his* Son hanging on the cross (Mark 15:34). She heard him gasp of his thirst—and she could do nothing. She heard him say, "Into your hands I commit My Spirit" (Luke 23:46), and she heard Jesus say, "It is finished" (John 19:30). This was a declaration of victory; He had finished his task and borne the wrath of God against all human sinfulness.

But Mary would not know that meaning yet. She only knew the life of her Son ended in unbearable agony and utter humiliation. What deep, inexpressible sorrow! And complete bewilderment! What about the promises? Was Jesus not, after all, the coming Savior, the Son of David? Had the promises failed? Was God's word not true? Could somehow this have been a terrible mistake from the very beginning? Her world had been rocked entirely off its foundations—again and more radically than ever before.

The Joy of the Resurrection

We do not know how Mary and Jesus' disciples spent the rest of that Passover eve and the following Sabbath. Their mourning had to be in secret. The men feared that the authorities would be after *them* as close friends and associates of Jesus. It was the women who went to the tomb in the early morning light. It was the women who discovered the stone rolled away. It was the women who saw the empty tomb and heard the angel's message that Jesus had risen. It was the women who *saw* Jesus and who heard him say he would meet them all in Galilee (Matt.28:1–7). And, although we are not told so in the Gospels, we can imagine Mary's boundless and unspeakable joy, as deep as her sorrow had been, as she saw finally the *real* end of the story and she knew what Jesus had meant when he said, "It is finished."

Mary is mentioned again in Acts 1:14, where she is singled out among the company of earnestly praying believers that also included the apostles, "the women" (implying those who had faithfully accompanied Jesus and his followers), and Jesus' brothers. The presence of her other sons in this group must have brought great joy to Mary who had seen their scorn and disbelief during Jesus' lifetime (John 7:1–5). This was now a healed family. Regarding the remainder of her life, church tradition tells us that she went with the apostle John to Ephesus and died there.

FURTHER REFLECTIONS

What can we learn from Mary's life, so ordinary and yet so extraordinary? While we need not make her an object of worship, her story of obedience and trust in the darkest hours is a model for us. Think of Mary having to manage the searing agony of the unjust death of her first child. We must ask ourselves how we have responded when our expectations and hopes for ourselves, or for those whom we love, have been utterly demolished.

Mary's faithfulness as God's servant did not come from her own strength, but from the power of the Word of God. She knew and trusted his great and precious promises that infuse the whole of the Old Testament. May we, regardless of heartbreaking sorrows and trying circumstances in our lives, commit ourselves to obedience, trust, and affirming that with God, nothing is impossible!

FIVE

Sarah and Hagar

BIBLICAL TEXTS: GENESIS 11:29–31; 12:1–20; 16:1–18:15;
20:1–21:21; 22:1–23:20; ROMANS 4:18–25

From Mary, we move back about 2000 years to Sarah, the wife of Abraham and the mother of God's chosen people. Her story intertwines at important points with that of her Egyptian slave woman, Hagar. At one level, the contrast between Mary and Sarah could not be more stark. Mary was young and poor; Sarah, when we first meet her in the pages of Genesis, was beautiful, privileged, and already middle-aged. Yet both would be vehicles for God's "impossible" works.

LEAVING HOME FOR A FOREIGN LAND

Sarah's name in its original form (Sarai) means "my princess," suggesting both a wealthy family background and perhaps parents for whom she was precious. Her name was later changed to Sarah (simply "princess") just as Abram's was changed to the better-known Abraham. Sarai first appears in Genesis 11:29–31 as Abram's wife and Terah's daughter-in-law. According to the customs of that day, Sarai would have brought a large dowry—from her well-to-do family—into her marriage with Abram.

At the age of sixty-five, she was comfortably middle-aged; she lived to be 127. Of all the matters that troubled her, the absence of children in her home would top the list. Her barrenness meant that the family name would not continue, a source of shame for both Abram and Sarai. In addition, just as her life was settling into the rhythms of middle age, Abram was called by God to leave home for an unknown land. She would, of course, be going along, leaving family, friends, familiar landscapes, and relative comforts in the city of Ur. Sarai would never see those places again. Those of us whose stable and comfortable existence has been suddenly uprooted by a career change, financial pressure, or some looming crisis know a bit of the emptiness that Sarai must have felt.

Sarai and Abram traveled north and then west, stopping for a while in a place called Haran. It seems that a good part of the extended family put down roots there, but Abram and Sarai set out again, because God said so. They headed south. Mountains and valleys, occasional oases, and nomadic tribes with their flocks all blended into the passing scenery. As they traveled, the languages changed and the customs were new. All that was certain was that God told Abram to get up and go, promising a family with countless descendants as well as land. God also declared that all nations would be blessed through Abram—whatever that might mean.

The prospects of children and land were beacons of hope, but once Sarai and Abram arrived in Canaan, it was not long before they had to pack up their tents again due to famine. This land was not like home had been, where the great Tigris and Euphrates rivers provided constant sources of water. This place was dependent on rainfall which sometimes failed, and the desert was too close for comfort. Imagine the family dynamics. Sarai continued to be barren; the land Abram was supposed to get was a disaster. Accusations and recriminations may have occasionally peppered their conversation, even as they tried valiantly to be faithful.

A THREATENED MARRIAGE: FIRST PHARAOH AND THEN
ABIMELECH

Abram and Sarai went on toward Egypt where the Nile River flowed without fail. Somewhere along the way, he likely said something like this: "We're obviously foreigners everywhere we go and that means we are targets. You're a beautiful woman—and I'm not just saying that. Worse yet, it's hard to cover up the fact that we've got lots of flocks and herds. These small-time rulers who want to expand their power and influence will take you, kill me, and enlarge their estates by calling all our possessions your 'dowry.' I've got a plan, however, to get around them. I am adopting you as my sister as well as having you as my wife. What that means to these kinglets is that you don't *have* a dowry if you are simply my sister. No one will dare to take you away without asking your brother's permission and I will never give it. Family ties run deep. So everywhere we go, you must say that you are my sister."

In Ancient Near Eastern culture, a brother could formally adopt a sister and Sarai was, in fact, a half-sister to Abram (Gen. 20:12). The adopted sister in this arrangement would not inherit from the brother and there was also no dowry to be expected. In other words, getting rid of Abram would not mean an easy profit to someone eyeing their prosperity. In fact, this may have been Abram's way of protecting his marriage, not jeopardizing Sarai's sexuality by making her "available." He says "that my life will be spared *for you*," not "because of you" (Gen. 12:13).[1]

It is vital to recognize that in Ancient Near Eastern culture, so grounded on honor, a man would not *give* his wife to another man; it would be utterly shameful. Pharaoh and later Abimelech were punished, implying they were in the wrong when they took what was not theirs. Sarai's obedience is commended in 1 Peter 3:1–6 and Peter seems to be referring to this situation. If this were an immoral decision, her obedience to Abram would not be praiseworthy.

The strategy worked until they came to Egypt. Pharaoh considered himself one of the gods of Egypt, representative of the sun god, Ra. Needless to say, what Pharaoh wanted, he got. When his officials praised Sarai's extraordinary beauty, he rejected the stated adoptive sister bond between Abram and Sarai and took her into his harem. He had, after all, all the power of Egypt and its gods. Abram was not even in the position to think about giving permission! Pharaoh did pay well for Sarai, but it was a wicked, long-term investment on his part. Because Sarai had no children, she was particularly attractive. All he had to do was to wait for this woman to die and he would inherit her wealth. In the meantime, she was a showpiece! Abimelech, king of the Philistines, later followed the same pattern, although it is notable that in that case, Sarah's beauty was not a stated issue. By that time, she was just about ninety years old and the main lure was the evident wealth of this family (Gen. 20:1–18).

Sarai's Deliverance from Pharaoh, Israel's Deliverance from Egypt

Sarai's time in the harem of Pharaoh was mercifully short because God intervened in a dramatic way. Plagues afflicted the Egyptian people and somehow Pharaoh came to understand that it was because of Sarai. She was immediately handed back and Abram was told to leave (Gen. 12:17–20).

In the deliverance of Sarai from Pharaoh, we are allowed to see a foreshadowing of the Exodus, the most significant event for all of God's people in the Old Testament. By means of plagues, a later Pharaoh would come to *know* that God was supremely powerful and also *very* jealous for his own "bride," Israel. Just as Abram and Sarai went away with their possessions radically increased, so also the Israelites would leave Egypt with all manner of wealth (Exod. 12:35-36), enough to build and furnish their own tabernacle, the place of worship that God would command them to build.

ARRANGING TO HAVE A SON THROUGH HAGAR

Still, Sarai had borne Abram no children. God had *promised*
Abram descendants, lots of them. Where was Sarai's place in this? She
felt helpless and sidelined. Ten years went by—"her womb was . . . dead"
(Rom. 4:19). How could she even believe God in these circumstances?
Children who had been born to her friends were now having children
of their own! She was 75. How difficult this was!

Sarai was a strong personality, and she took the matter into her
own hands. In her culture, a woman who was unable to have children
could adopt as her own any child born in her tent. A slave could serve
as a surrogate mother. Hagar, a young woman who had been added to
the family property while they were in Egypt, was Sarai's choice for this
role. Hagar probably did not have anything to say about the matter.

At Sarai's urging, Abram slept with Hagar who immediately conceived a child. How humiliating! Sarai had spent the last ten years
trying with Abram to fulfill that part of God's promise and she was
undone by her handmaid's success practically overnight. How very
bitter were the outcomes, many of them unfolding over years to come!

MORE THREATS TO THE MARRIAGE: JEALOUSY, BITTERNESS, AND CRUELTY

Wounded pride, contempt, and cruelty. There was open hostility
between these two women and Sarai's anger turned back on Abram as
she berated him for fulfilling her intentions! Abram washed his hands
of the affair and refused to do anything to stop Sarai's subsequent
abuse of Hagar. Both Sarai and Hagar had endured so much already
because of circumstances outside their control, and they made each
other suffer even more through their arrogance, cruel comments, and
harsh treatment of one another (Gen. 16:4–6).

Hagar was in a powerful position. She had *everything* Sarai wanted—
and she knew it—and wielded that power in a devastating way. Likewise,
Sarai abused the power of her status. It was the only thing she knew to

do—make Hagar's *pleasure* in being a mother the most miserable thing possible. In doing so and eventually driving Hagar away, she was driving away what she wanted the most—a child!

HAGAR'S FLIGHT: TO THE PROVISION OF GOD

When Hagar ran away, she headed for Egypt, for home. It was a desperate choice. The way was long and truly impossible for a woman alone. How would she find food and water in the barrenness of the wilderness? What about roaming bands of shiftless and evil characters? As she stopped at "the spring on the way to Shur" (Gen. 16:7), the angel of the Lord met her. How heartening it must have been to be addressed by name, but how unnerving at the same time! The angel knew she was Sarai's servant, which meant he knew she was on the run. His question was designed to get a confession out of her.

Without excuses or voicing any of the injustice she had suffered, Hagar declared that she was fleeing, apparently trusting this messenger to know the rest of her story. As he commanded her to go back and submit to Sarai, he gave her the strength and courage to do so. We can only wonder at the profound sense of God's presence that turned her past bitterness and anger to confession and submission. And we can pray for that abiding presence for ourselves in those equally trying times when we are fleeing in anger from people and circumstances that fill our hearts to the breaking point.

Hagar's son was to be named Ishmael, meaning *God hears*. And Hagar knew that the One who met her was also the God who *sees* and *provides*. Although we are not told of her feelings, we can imagine what it meant for Hagar to humble herself, ask to be part of the household again, maintain a quiet demeanor, and birth the son who so distressed Sarai.

Let us also imagine a small sampling of what Sarai had been thinking after Hagar left. Perhaps there was a steady drumbeat of remorse and self-recrimination for not being able to rise above the emotional tangle caused by Hagar's contempt. She had not expected that at all when she masterminded the situation. Her plan was according to an accepted custom, but resulted in such intense frustration and insults that the fabric of her family unraveled. She had given her husband to another woman to have this child, a child she was certain was the fulfillment of God's promise. How else could it be arranged? Did Sarai feel guilt at the way she had treated Hagar? Maybe. During that time, no doubt God gave her courage and strength as well—the strength of character to face a bad situation that she had created, and make it work as well as possible.

HAGAR'S RETURN AND THE BIRTH OF ISHMAEL

Both Sarai and Hagar were flawed human beings and the same pride and pain were still there after Hagar returned. Ishmael was born into that home—which meant the tensions would increase. Ishmael was Abram's first born son. Abram loved him and actually wanted him to be the promised son—to get the waiting over with. How long, after all, would God make them wait? And what other difficulties would they get themselves into by trying, to the best of their ability, to *find* God's way and fulfill his promises?

VISITED BY ANGELS: WITH GOD NOTHING IS IMPOSSIBLE

How many ways we all have of trying to nudge along the purposes of God! How quickly we want things made right—which often means right according to our own purposes and intentions. Abram and Sarai waited twenty-five years from the first promise to the birth of Isaac. That's one whole generation that passed them by. How painfully their hopes of Sarai's bearing a child must have dwindled! How they must have wracked their brains trying to figure out other ways God might make it happen!

In the course of those years, God directed them to change their names (Gen. 17:5, 15). At the time, Abram was ninety-nine; Sarai was ten years younger. Abram ("exalted father") would be called Abraham ("father of a multitude"), a public testimony to God's promise, but one that might have caused some ridicule from his friends and neighbors! In fact, Abraham himself was incredulous and laughed at the prospect to which God simply said, "It will be Sarah who will have a son and you will call his name Laughter (Isaac). It's going to happen next year" (Gen. 17:19–21). At the same time, Sarai's name ("my princess") was changed to Sarah, simply meaning "princess." By this time, she was an old princess. As she put it, she was "worn out" and no longer in any condition to conceive a child.

But one day, Abraham entertained three visitors (Gen. 18:1–15). When they arrived in the heat of the day, he was quick to engage Sarah in the preparation of a feast. It was a matter of hospitality, even though the temperature was likely well over 100 degrees. Even under those conditions, Sarah baked the bread; he prepared a whole calf. No microwaves or air conditioning! By the time the meal was ready, evening had no doubt come and they ate outside under a tree where it would be cooler. Abraham took the posture of a servant, standing beside them. Sarah stayed in the tent.

After eating, the first topic of discussion was Sarah. One of the visitors asked Abraham, "Where is your wife?" knowing full well, since it was the Lord speaking, that she was in the tent listening intently to their conversation. His message, presumably directed to Abraham, was equally meant for Sarah. She had followed Abraham's cues and recognized that these were no ordinary visitors. After all, Abraham had bowed low to the ground when they first arrived. Therefore, her ears were ready. Yet what she heard caused her to laugh so hard she could hardly contain herself. The primary speaker of the three, identified as the Lord, said "Next year your wife Sarah will have a son." This was what they wanted and had been waiting and longing for, but now it was way too late. She was *old*, too old to have a child. This was a bad joke. But to her horror, the next thing she heard the visitor say was "Why did Sarah laugh and say 'Will

I really have a child now that I am old?'" How did he know? Who was this anyway? This was not only embarrassing; it was unnerving! And his next statement was, "Is anything too difficult for the LORD?" That, too, was for her benefit as well as Abraham's.

Both of them had laughed at the announcement that it would be Sarah, now in her old age, who would bear the child. In Chapter 1, we read that Mary also heard an angel say "with God nothing is impossible." Here was the same assurance. Nothing, nothing at all is too difficult for the Lord.

But at that moment, Sarah was afraid. To get out of an uncomfortable situation, she did what many of us do. She lied outright and said, "I did not laugh." "Ah, but you did," the visitor replied. And that was the end of the Lord's communication with her. Her laughter born of disbelief joined Abraham's. Yet from their skeptical laughter would come the name for their son. Just as the Lord had promised, Sarah bore a son to Abraham.

ROMANS 4:18–25: GOD HAS THE POWER TO DO WHAT HE SAYS HE WILL DO

Abraham's faith was a favorite subject of Paul. In Romans 4, he refers directly to Sarah's barrenness as part of the discussion. In spite of all the biological evidence to the contrary, Abraham was "fully convinced" that God had the power to do what he said he would do. Even though it took a painfully long time; even though Abraham and Sarah were at intervals skeptical and incredulous, they came to *believe* the Word of God and trust in his promises. Paul's point is that this incident was not solely for the strengthening of Abraham and Sarah in their faith; we, too, can know that the God who raised Jesus from the dead is fully trustworthy as he will do what he has promised.

HAGAR AND ISHMAEL FINALLY SENT AWAY

Abraham and Sarah did name the child Isaac and she declared, "God has brought me laughter and everyone who hears about this will laugh with me" (Gen. 21:6). This time the laughter was not incredulous; it was the utter joy that comes when something seemingly impossible becomes reality. And everyone joined the celebration. Everyone, that is, except Hagar and her son, Ishmael. The tension that had existed between Sarah and Hagar resurfaced between Ishmael and Isaac. When Sarah saw Ishmael, some fourteen years older than Isaac, mocking the celebration of Isaac's weaning, she told Abraham to send Hagar and Ishmael away (Gen. 21:8–10).

This was a bold demand and it was cruel to Abraham. Although Sarah deeply disliked Hagar and Ishmael, Ishmael was Abraham's own son. Sarah's demand troubled him. Nevertheless, the Lord himself told Abraham to do as Sarah said. It's an interesting lesson: Sarah's demand sounds very selfish and her motives were probably anything but pure. Even so, it was the right thing to do. God had made it clear that Isaac was the son who would be Abraham's heir. The longer Ishmael was present, the more potentially ugly the whole scene could become. At the same time, God reassured Abraham about Ishmael's future, declaring that Hagar's son would be the father of a nation as well (Gen. 21:13).

So Hagar left, sent off with some bread and a skin flask of water. What a bitter parting! Hagar's son *was* the firstborn, and she was told when Abraham fathered the child that it was in order to build Abraham's family. Now, more than a decade later, they were put out of the tent with nothing. Abraham must have felt overwhelmed, but he had to obey the Lord who had affirmed Sarah's demand.

In Genesis 21:14, we read that Hagar wandered in the desert of Beersheba—hot, dry, and desolate. It was similar to the deadly wilderness where she had ended up fifteen years earlier. But this time, she had her son with her. When the skin flask of water was slack and empty, she despaired. She "flung" Ishmael under a bush and sat some distance away, for she could not bear to watch him die. Ishmael would have been almost fifteen years old, but had not been toughened as his mother had by her years as a house slave. Hagar wept bitterly; her son was dying. Everything in her life had completely fallen apart and she could do nothing to save either her son or herself.

In this hopeless place, the angel of God called to her and told her not to be afraid, but to take the boy up and lead him by the hand. Hagar was obedient to that call and, in the moment where she had come to her complete end, where she had nothing left, God again provided. They needed water; God provided a well.

Hagar and Ishmael continued to live in that desert area, in a place called the Desert of Paran, farther south than Beersheba where the angel of the Lord had met their needs. Hagar found a wife for Ishmael from Egypt, re-establishing connections with her own homeland and people. In that cultural context, the growing family network would provide for her as she grew older. Nevertheless, that social structure would not make up for the gnawing emptiness in her life. She had been used in what turned out to be misguided purposes. When it was apparent that they were misguided, she was driven away in hatred and fury. How can we fathom that? What's more, how can we fathom her uncomplaining obedience, first to Sarah's demands and then to the Lord's even more demanding word: Go back! Endure some more! In spite of the raw tragedy of which she was the central character, she knew God saw her, and provided. And that was enough.

THE LAST TEST

Sarah's home life became more peaceful; the thorns of taunting from Ishmael and sullen service from Hagar were gone. God, however, had a way of upending life and ripping away any potential complacency. The Bible says that God tested Abraham, but this trial would cause just as much, perhaps even more, anguish for Sarah; Isaac was her *only* son. The silence is deafening; we read nothing of her part in the ordeal.

After all the family ties with Ishmael had been broken, God told Abraham to take his son, his only son, Isaac, whom he loved, and go to the region of Moriah. There Abraham was to sacrifice Isaac as a burnt offering. Mere words flatten the horror of this drama. God's command meant slaughtering Isaac, a ritual Abraham would have to perform with a knife in his hand. Then he would have to watch the body of Isaac engulfed by a flaming fire on an altar that he would construct. It was too appalling. God had promised that through Isaac, Abraham and Sarah would have many descendants. That was God's word, and now Abraham heard another word, the command to kill this only son.

We only know that Abraham got up early the next morning, prepared wood for the burnt offering, and set out with two servants. Did he tell Sarah? Or was he too afraid of her response? Sarah was a forceful person, and yet here we read nothing about her. If she knew, perhaps she considered it punishment for her treatment of Hagar and Ishmael. We can only imagine the conflicted horror of self-torment, anger at Abraham, and utter bewilderment at the God who made such promises and demands. Perhaps she tried to persuade Abraham not to go, that this could not possibly be God's command. If Isaac was killed, would that mean the plan went back to Ishmael? That she could not bear. She may have urged Abraham to stop, but this time she would not prevail. Abraham left with the servants and Isaac.

On the third day, they arrived at the awful place, Moriah. Abraham left the servants while he and Isaac went on ahead. Isaac asked where the animal for the burnt offering was and all Abraham could say was, "The Lord will provide," the same promise Hagar found to be true. The Lord would provide. Abraham did not know how else to explain it. He bound Isaac, who did not resist even though he was no longer a small child. Abraham was lifting up the knife to plunge it into the young man when the angel of the Lord stopped him. The angel declared that now he knew that Abraham feared the Lord. The Lord *provided* a ram for the sacrifice, and promised that he would bless Abraham and his descendants. Abraham had passed this severe test. So had Isaac. But what about Sarah?

Abraham and the servants returned to Beersheba, "and Abraham stayed in Beersheba" (Gen. 22:19). There is no mention of Isaac accompanying them on this journey—we do not know why. When Isaac was 37, Sarah died at the age of 127, and she died at a place called Kiriath Arba, also called Hebron. It is about a day's journey north of Beersheba. Did Abraham and Sarah live apart after that terrible event? It is possible. The text tells us that Abraham came to mourn over her and purchased land to bury her. This purchase was the first small step toward the fulfillment of God's covenant promise that Abraham's descendants would possess the Promised Land. It took Sarah's death to see that part of the promise even begin to move toward fulfillment.

FURTHER REFLECTIONS

Sarah is an interesting study; she submitted to Abram's plan to adopt her as his sister, and yet she was sufficiently forceful to prevail over him in each exchange that involved Hagar. Perhaps this illustrates something of the immense power of maternal desires in close conjunction with jealousy. At the same time, Sarah had to accept Hagar back into her household and make it work. Likewise, we often are compelled to live with irritating people and circumstances that vex us deeply. What strategies can we employ to learn grace, patience, and forgiveness? One of the steady themes through all of Sarah's life is the evidence of God's loving and perfect purposes overriding imperfect human efforts. If we can begin to wrap our minds around the implications of God's sovereignty as He does indeed work *everything* for good (Rom. 8:28), we will nurture the ability to forgive the wrongs that *are* part of life. In fact, this is the only way to combat the growing bitterness that otherwise gnaws away our joy. Those of us who consistently reduce God to our own limited imaginations and capabilities will do well to revisit this truth—many times.

For her part, Hagar was driven away into utter desolation in order to be found by God. When we come to the very end of our own strength on our journeys, God will provide. He may simply provide more strength, more courage, comfort in the midst of deep sorrow, patience to deal with one more agonizingly repetitive question, freedom from fear, another day's worth of food and water, but we can trust that he will provide what we need. This is easy to write—and to read. It is exceedingly more difficult to believe with all of our hearts and accordingly to act in obedience.

Sarah's life was filled with disappointment and laughter, bitter envy and longing, fear and vindication. She questioned God, not always knowing whom she was confronting. How like us! Sarah wrestled with the consequences of decisions that seemed to be logical, and yet were so wrong. Our lives often echo that familiar pattern. She had to deal with jealousy, disbelief, and anguish over her son. All of these emotions resonate with each one of us far more often than we care to acknowledge.

Like Mary, Sarah was told that nothing is impossible with God. In each case, the seemingly impossible was indeed beyond the reaches of natural processes. These were impossible events until God intervened. May our faith be strong enough to believe that God's power will indeed accomplish God's loving purposes and fulfill His promises!

1 This is a radically different interpretation of this incident and I am indebted to Gordon Hugenberger, senior pastor emeritus of Park Street Church in Boston, MA, for tying the biblical material together in a most compelling and coherent manner.

SIX

Rebekah, Leah, and Rachel

BIBLICAL TEXTS: GENESIS 24:1–67; 25:19–34;
27:1 THROUGH 31:55

There is a strong echo of Sarah's continuing presence when we read that Isaac married Rebekah and " . . . brought her into the tent of his mother Sarah . . ." (Gen. 24:67). Everyone leaves memories that are etched into and shape the lives of those who follow.

Each subsequent matriarch of Israel planted her own character firmly in the pages of Scripture and no doubt firmly in the family lore as well. They were wise, energetic, and cleverly manipulative, as well as deeply wounded and scarred. Nevertheless, God used their brokenness, jealousy, and frustration to accomplish his purposes.

REBEKAH'S STRENGTH OF CHARACTER

Sarah's daughter-in-law, Rebekah, came from Paddan Aram, which might be like saying she came to Ohio from Massachusetts. Paddan Aram was the region of northwest Mesopotamia where Abraham's family temporarily lived as they migrated westward. A good number of the extended family had stayed there when Sarah and Abraham had heeded God's call to continue on to Canaan. It was a long distance from Beersheba where Abraham and Isaac were living after burying Sarah, but Abraham was intent on acquiring a wife for Isaac from among his own people.

Rebekah came to be Isaac's wife without ever having seen him! She had only heard Abraham's servant tell a story that went like this: "Because I have served Abraham faithfully for such a long time—he is quite old now, you know—he entrusted me with a very important task. In fact, he made me take a solemn vow that I would find a wife for Isaac in 'the old country' and bring her back to live in the land God promised to Abraham. Isaac is his only son, and he was quite particular that I was not to bring him back here—ever. So, I set off with ten camels and when I finally arrived in your town, I stopped at the well in the evening. It was cooler by that time and the young women were carrying water for the next day's needs. Not quite sure what to do on my own, I prayed a very specific prayer. It was bold! I asked that the girl I approached for a drink would respond by offering to water my camels as well. I need to tell you that I'd been traveling with ten camels and they had not had water for quite some time. Praise be! God honored my prayer even before I finished it! Rebekah here came out carrying her jar and she was very polite as she gave me a drink. Then she really did offer to water all the camels and ran back and forth filling the water trough from her jug, more than twenty jugs full for each camel! I watched her carefully; this must be the one. It could not have been a more clear answer. When she finished, I asked who she was and she kindly offered your hospitality. You know the rest." (Gen. 24:1–49).

Hearing this remarkable answer to prayer, Rebekah's father and brother acknowledged that it was from the Lord and immediately told the servant to take her and go! There was a grand celebration that night and the next morning, the servant was ready to depart. Rebekah actually agreed to set off at once on this journey even though her brother and mother wanted her to wait ten days. We are not told how she felt about this. It was expected that she would go without question; the only issue for her was how much time she would have to say goodbye to everything and everyone she had known all her life.

Think for a moment. No matter what decision faces us, we often have an over-abundance of options from which to choose. In fact, sometimes the sheer number of possibilities is overwhelming. We get busy making lists of "pros" and "cons," praying through those lists, asking which is "God's will," and seeking advice. Rebecca had only two choices and it is doubtful that either of them was how she had imagined her life unfolding. Isn't it interesting that she chose the one that was the less "comfortable" and comforting? And then away she went (Gen. 24:50–61)!

No doubt there was sizable group of attendants on the return trip as Rebekah would hardly have travelled without servants and women to accompany her to an entirely strange land. After the long journey, they arrived near Beersheba in the southern part of Canaan. Just as Sarah may have hesitated at the inhospitable land where she arrived with Abraham, so also Rebekah must have paused as she surveyed the barren wilderness around Beersheba. What on earth had she gotten herself into? We have, however, no record of her dismay.

Isaac, walking in the field, "lifted up his eyes" and saw the camels coming. Rebekah likewise "lifted up her eyes," saw him, and descended from the camel. When she learned it was Isaac, she modestly retreated behind her veil as the servant told him the whole story, no doubt to assure him that she was clearly the right woman. He took her as his wife into his mother's tent and the Bible says that he loved her (Gen.24:62–67). There was no prior courtship, no decision to make as to whether they were "right for each other." God had arranged this marriage and Isaac invested in it right from the start. In a particularly tender way, the story closes with the affirmation that Isaac was comforted after his mother's death by his marriage to Rebekah.

Mother of Esau and Jacob

Like Sarah, Rebekah also suffered through years of waiting for children. In fact, Isaac prayed for his wife for twenty long years, knowing both her grief and the nagging awareness of the promise God had made to Abraham. This family was supposed to be *large* and here they were again—not able to begin the process for this generation. Surely the memory of his own mother's narrative would compel Isaac to continue to pray. After all, Rebekah was much younger. Sarah had finally conceived at the age of ninety. Rebekah's pregnancy would not be impossible for God!

When both Sarah and Rebekah finally bore children, it was testimony to God's sovereign intervention in the way and time he designed. In this case, Rebekah was carrying twins. The struggles that would characterize the relationship between her sons started while they were yet unborn. They were, we might say, fighting in her womb! Troubled, Rebekah went to ask the Lord what was happening. It was not only Isaac who prayed. In fact, while we have no verbal record of God's responding to Isaac, we do know what God said to Rebekah: "Two nations are in your womb, and two peoples from within you will be separated; one people will be stronger than the other, and the older will serve the younger" (Gen. 25:23).

In this verse, God chose to speak prophetically through Rebekah. The last line is the most significant, both foretelling their dysfunctional family narrative, and bearing far-reaching theological implications as well. Almost two millennia later, the apostle Paul quoted this prophecy to emphasize that it is God and no one else who determines who His children will be. Before the boys were born and able to make any decisions on their own, God declared His plan. Neither Jacob nor any of his descendants could ever say that it was because of the good things they had done or the choices they made that they were favored as children of God (Rom. 9:10–12).

REBEKAH'S SCHEME: BLESSING FOR JACOB INSTEAD OF ESAU

Rebekah's twins were Esau, who was born first, and Jacob. Each had distinctive character traits that clashed as they got older. Rebekah and Isaac gave Jacob his name because he was clutching his brother's heel as they were born. This foreshadowed the nature of their ongoing interactions, with Jacob striving to overtake Esau. Early on, Jacob seemed to be more calculating; Esau more impulsive. Now that's a familiar parental challenge!

This dynamic was made particularly clear one day when Esau returned from hunting. He claimed to be famished and demanded some of the red stew Jacob was cooking, lest he expire on the spot. (There might have been a bit of the melodramatic in Esau.) Jacob shrewdly made him vow to give over the birthright before he handed along the pot of stew. It could be that Jacob knew the prophecy from his mother and was conniving in order to bring it about himself. The birthright normally went to the firstborn son and meant particular honor as well as a double portion of the family inheritance in order to provide care for the whole household. Both sons were culpable in this incident; the Bible says that Esau despised his birthright (Gen. 25:34; see also Heb. 12:16-17). But Jacob was grasping at it.

Favoritism contributed further to the uneasy family dynamics. Rebekah evidently favored Jacob, no doubt because of the prophetic declaration regarding his future. She loved him, and may have kept him closer to home to protect him. Esau roamed freely, hunting and bringing home good food to eat. His activities appealed especially to Isaac, who loved his firstborn son.

Love for children is an odd thing. Some connections are just closer, no matter how hard parents try to keep a balance. Isaac's love for Esau was understandable at one level; he was his firstborn son and he liked Esau's strength and active life. Isaac was going blind and perhaps he was experiencing vicariously through his son the things he had enjoyed and could no longer do. There is also a symbolic aspect to his blindness. In spite of the prophetic word about the two sons, Isaac deliberately set up a ceremony in which he intended to pronounce the blessing on Esau. More on that incident and the content of Isaac's blessing shortly!

In Isaac's defense, we might suggest that Rebekah never told him the nature of the Lord's message to her. Perhaps it was not the custom to speak of such things. Perhaps even to propose that the firstborn would serve the younger was so preposterous that she never dared to utter the words to Isaac. Having posed that possibility, however, there is a hint in the wider narrative that their relationship was sufficiently intimate and this matter was sufficiently important that Rebekah would indeed have told Isaac about the Lord's response to her prayer.

Shortly after the birth of the twins, the family was living in the region controlled by a local ruler named Abimelech. Noting that Rebekah was beautiful, the local men asked Isaac about her and, following his father's pattern, he declared she was his sister. Who knows why he did that! Perhaps because it had worked so well for Abraham. At any rate, all was going well until Abimelech saw Isaac "playing" with Rebekah. The Hebrew word is the same one from which Isaac's name comes. It means to laugh, play, enjoy—whatever they were doing, Abimelech *knew* they were married (Gen. 26:8–9)! Their behavior reflected personal intimacy. That would suggest they also shared the knowledge of that momentous prophetic statement, especially since Isaac had actively been praying for Rebekah to have children for twenty years. This was of utmost importance to both of them.

What happened in the interval between those events and the incident we are about to narrate? Decades had elapsed. The twins were now forty years old. Esau had married Canaanite women who made life miserable for both Isaac and Rebekah. Isaac had gone blind and was confined at home. We might imagine Rebekah, at least twenty years his junior, slowly but surely assuming more management of the estate. It may be that, of the twins, Jacob was the more dependable and was assisting Rebekah as Isaac grew less able to oversee an extensive household and the flocks and herds. In spite of the family distress with Esau's Canaanite wives, however, there came a day when Isaac determined to bless Esau (Gen. 27:1–4).

Just as Sarah had listened at the tent door, so also Rebekah. And what she heard catapulted her into action; Isaac was concocting a ceremony during which he would savor a special meal provided by Esau and then bless Esau in return. This was not an informal occasion. Concluding that the prophetic statement about Jacob was about to be permanently thwarted, Rebekah persuaded Jacob to dress like Esau and bring a good stew that Rebekah herself would cook. Even though Jacob protested, Rebekah told him to obey her, taking on herself the responsibility for the outcome. It was a daring and even reckless plan. Isaac was blind, but that did not mean he was senseless. In fact, his senses of smell and touch would be keener than ever and Jacob did not smell of the outdoors, nor was he rough and hairy like his brother. That meant the disguise had to go beyond simple clothing; Rebekah covered Jacob's smooth skin with goatskins (Gen. 27:5–17).

What a dilemma Rebekah confronted at this point! God's promise was in danger of being broken by the obstinate determination of her elderly, blind husband. Was she to stand idly by? Or should she stop Isaac's rash scheme at all costs? How would she continue to live with Isaac's anger at being duped when he found out? Would they be at loggerheads for the rest of their marriage? When Jacob came to his father and Isaac spoke to the person he thought was Esau, he used words that would clearly set Esau above his brother, "Be master over your brothers; may your mother's sons bow down to you." In God's providence and with Rebekah's shrewd manipulation, that declaration was indeed made to Jacob instead of Esau.

All parties in this dysfunctional family contributed generously to the mess that resulted. Rebekah and Jacob tricked Isaac, who was then furious and possibly frightened when Esau returned seeking the same blessing. The narrative says that Isaac "trembled." Tragically, after all Rebekah's effort to make the prophecy turn out the way she thought it was supposed to, Esau was so angry that Jacob had to flee for his life. Rebekah heard his murderous threats and again summoned her favorite son and commanded his obedience; he was to head for her homeland and stay there until she told him it was safe to return (Gen. 27:42–45).

As far as we know, that message never came; there is no indication in the story that Rebekah ever saw her younger and favorite son again. In fact, nothing is said about her at all after this incident, only that her nurse died and was buried near Bethel. The nurse, whose name was Deborah, had probably seen and heard much of the pain her mistress suffered during these years. Isaac, by the way, who had told Esau he was about to die when he arranged the whole blessing scene, lived to be 180 and was buried by Esau and Jacob after Jacob's return to the land several decades later.

DIFFICULT CHOICES, PAINFUL RESULTS

Rebekah's quandary echoed some aspects of Sarah's dilemma. Sarah and Abraham did their best to "arrange" for the fulfillment of God's promise of a son, but their "arrangement" painfully complicated the lives of others. Likewise, Rebekah tried to the best of her ability to make certain that Isaac did not do something contrary to the will of the Lord. Fully aware of God's stated plans, Sarah and Rebekah made choices that brought anguish to themselves and to others around them because they did not know how he would accomplish his purposes. Or perhaps they did not have a large enough picture of the power and wisdom of God.

Occasionally our great sins are committed with the "best of intentions," but most of the time they are committed as we pursue selfish desires. No doubt there were selfish motives creeping into each of these women's hearts as well. Sarah so deeply wanted a son, and she wanted sole rights with no competition from anyone else, notably Ishmael, the son of a handmaid. Rebekah loved Jacob, fiercely protected him, and even controlled him. These emotions were as powerful as her commitment to seeing the prophecy fulfilled.

LEAH, RACHEL, AND THEIR HOUSEHOLD

Although Jacob fled from home alone, when he returned years later he had two wives, Leah and Rachel, as well as their handmaids, Bilhah and Zilpah. Leah and Rachel were sisters who fought jealously for the love of their husband. Here again, it seems that God "took sides."

From the outset, Jacob loved Rachel more. In fact, he initially asked to marry her in exchange for seven years of labor but had been duped by her father, Laban, who cunningly substituted his less attractive older daughter on the wedding night. It was not a good way to start. Agreeing to another seven years, Jacob also won his beloved Rachel (Gen. 29:15–30). Rachel, however, was barren, by now a familiar pattern.

As Leah had children, each was named as triumphant recognition that God had favored her. At the same time, her reasons for the names expressed a deep aching for love. Her firstborn was named Reuben, meaning that God had *seen* her misery and given her a son; surely that would compel Jacob to love her. Simeon's name added the sense of sound; God had *heard* her cry for love. Levi and Judah also bore names that drew together her yearning for Jacob's love and her joy at God's bounty. Levi is related to a Hebrew word that may mean "joined" or "accompanying," while the word for "praise" underlies the name Judah. The names no doubt also served as in-your-face reminders to Rachel that she was a failure in this role. Therefore, Rachel's handmaid Bilhah was given over as a surrogate mother and she bore two sons, causing Rachel to claim a victory. Not to be outdone, Leah pressed Zilpah into service to stay ahead in the childbearing tally.

After years of waiting and longing, Rachel finally bore her son

Joseph. Eventually she would also give birth to Benjamin, but lose her life in the process.

Both Leah and Rachel were consumed with envy. Leah envied the love that Rachel shared with Jacob; Rachel envied the ease with which Leah was able to have children. Nevertheless, between these two women and their handmaids, Jacob fathered the twelve sons whose descendants would become the twelve tribes of Israel.

What's more, as the family grew older, perhaps wiser, Leah and Rachel stuck together. When Jacob decided to leave Laban and explained his reasons, the sisters were of one voice. No competition and jealousy now. Reading between the lines, it seems that Laban had been a scoundrel all the way around, trying to cheat them out of their dowries. They were more than willing to leave and go where God would lead Jacob.

In one final jab at Laban, Rachel stole his household gods as they were leaving and, through a clever ruse, managed to avoid being found out. This episode was complicated; we cheer for Rachel as she outfoxed her deceitful and conniving father, and yet she too was lying. It's a tragic characteristic that threads its way through these narratives about Jacob's family.

FURTHER REFLECTIONS

How shall we draw these thoughts together? Above all, we again come face to face with the abiding truth that God will accomplish his good purposes no matter what the circumstances. Furthermore, our job is to trust him to do so—even when those circumstances seem impossibly complicated. This was true for Rebekah as she left home. Her options as a beautiful young woman whose father and brother recognized an advantageous match were slim; she could go with Abraham's servant right away or ten days later! In trusting obedience, she went right away. That same innocent trust was not evident when she encountered head-on Isaac's blind choice to bless Esau. She was older, but perhaps not wiser! In that case, her attempt to intervene had tragic consequences for both her sons.

As Leah and Rachel wrestled with jealousy and unwieldy family dynamics, they were likely not focused on God's perfect purposes for the generations of descendants who would become Israel. How like us as we muddle through the messy situations in life; it is difficult to get the long view perspective. We, however, have the privilege of looking back through the lens of Scripture and can see a shining pattern— God is unfailingly faithful and he uses sinful, struggling people to accomplish his purposes.

SEVEN

God's Plan Included
Foreign Women

BIBLICAL TEXTS: GENESIS 37, 39–50; EXODUS 1–4;
JOSHUA 2, 6 ; HEBREWS 11; JAMES 2 :14–26

I t's all too easy to stand at the hedge around our church communities and look with a good deal of suspicion at everyone who obviously does not "belong." We are afraid and become unsettled with different ways of thinking, speaking, dressing, and acting. To protect our identity, we create a narrow field in which to live.

By way of contrast, God's majestic design included Egyptian women, the daughter of a Midianite priest, and a very bold Canaanite living in Jericho. These women crossed class boundaries—from the wife of an Egyptian official as well as the daughter of Pharaoh, to a prostitute who offered a safe hiding place to Israelites. Many of these women were exemplary and courageous; some were not. No surprise there! And by the way, we're saving Ruth for later; she gets her own chapter.

One more introductory matter: Because the most significant event in all of Israelite history was the Passover and Exodus from Egypt, we need to briefly remind ourselves how they got to Egypt in the first place. That means turning our attention to Joseph. Thirteen chapters at the end of Genesis are given to his story and from them we learn remarkable lessons.

THE ROLE OF AN EGYPTIAN SEDUCTRESS

Joseph's story line has an abundance of detail about a hate-filled and vindictive family that is in the very long and slow process of restoration. In those agonizingly slow steps toward forgiveness and responsibility, we also hear hints, uttered by Joseph himself, that God had purposes extending far beyond his own lifetime. We shall return to those purposes shortly.

After years of barrenness, Rachel bore Joseph and, because she was Jacob's favored wife, Joseph was Jacob's favorite son. The ugly pattern from the family of Isaac and Rebekah repeated itself in this generation as well. Joseph's half-brothers absolutely hated him, and it was not entirely without cause. As a teenager, Joseph had a strong arrogant streak about him and he was not afraid to flaunt his own superior position by wearing the special robe Jacob had given him and by telling his self-exalting dreams. No matter that the dreams would turn out to be true; at this point, they were inflammatory! He even dreamt of his mother, long since dead, bowing down to him along with his father and the assortment of half-brothers.

The upshot of it all was that these half-brothers sold him to a caravan of spice traders on their way to Egypt and agreed to a cover-up that made them look entirely innocent—the blood-soaked robe, the ever-present threat of wild animals. The problem was that they had to live with their lie for twenty years, and then come face-to-face with Joseph, who first terrorized them with his own elaborate deception.

An Egyptian officer of Pharaoh named Potiphar bought Joseph and, seeing how capable he was, put him in charge of his household. All was well and good. In fact, things were going better than Joseph could ever have expected after the dreadful betrayal by his brothers, except that he was way too good-looking and Potiphar's wife was smitten with him. She may have been accustomed to getting her way, but in this case she did not. As a result, Joseph's intent to flee sexual temptation cost him his position and his freedom, both no doubt very precious to him after what he had already been through.

Having been rebuffed by Joseph, Potiphar's wife told a bald-faced lie that landed Joseph in prison. What utter injustice! How could God set him up in such hopeful circumstances only to dash them completely? But it was this action that brought Joseph into contact with the person who would commend him to Pharaoh two years later. And it was his God-given ability to interpret dreams that brought him favor with Pharaoh and a post as second-in-command over all of Egypt. And that set the stage for the arrival of all of his brothers and their families into Egypt.

When Joseph addressed his brothers twenty years after their treachery against him, they had every reason to be fearful. He had been transformed from their little brother to a powerful ruler. Yet he affirmed God's purposes, saying it was God who sent him ahead of them (Gen. 45:5–8) to preserve them. He reassured them that he knew God had meant all of those bitter circumstances for good (Gen. 50:15–21). One of those was his undeserved sojourn in prison because of the false testimony of Potiphar's wife, and he had gotten to that low point as the result of his brothers' duplicity. A lesson—and it is a very important one: Love and forgiveness that build on the affirmation of God's sovereignty are the only antidotes to the ugly thorns of bitterness and resentment.

EGYPTIAN MIDWIVES

Between the close of Genesis and the move of Joseph's family into Egypt and Exodus 1, four hundred years elapsed. During this time, the position of the Israelites had changed drastically for the worse. To be sure, they had multiplied into a formidable force, but their very numbers were threatening to the king of Egypt. Whoever this king was—and we do not know the identity of the pharaoh—he had no regard for Joseph. All he saw was a growing slave population that was potentially dangerous. He was in an odd position. He needed their labor to keep the agricultural and religious economies going, but he also had to control their population explosion so that they would not become sufficiently large to threaten political stability (Exod. 1:10). Therefore, he first oppressed them with harsh construction and field labor. He declared that he would "deal shrewdly" with them, but each tactic was a dismal failure!

When the ruthless exploitation did not work, he ordered the midwives, Shiphrah and Puah, to kill baby boys as they were born (Exod. 1:16). In other words, the decree from the top was infanticide. It was not the last time this murderous tactic has been used to reduce population numbers. These good women, however, feared God and refused to do the king's bidding. It is not certain whether they were Hebrew or Egyptian, but the latter seems more likely.

When Pharaoh summoned them, no doubt in order to execute them for disobedience, they had a great excuse ready. Unlike the soft and pampered Egyptian women who needed the attention of a midwife, the Hebrew women gave birth vigorously and on their own. Were they telling a lie? Probably. But God blessed those midwives because they valued life, giving them families of their own. The title Pharaoh means "great house." Ironically, the word translated "families" in the scriptural account is literally "houses." God gave these midwives "houses." Furthermore, they have been named and honored through the succeeding millennia. We do not even know the name of this king of Egypt—he simply bears an anonymous title.

PHARAOH'S DAUGHTER

Frustrated in his prior attempts to control the Hebrew slave population, Pharaoh decreed that all baby boys were to be thrown into the Nile River. It was in the context of that murderous order that the baby Moses was rescued by Pharaoh's daughter. What audacity! She directly disobeyed her father's edict, which meant she countered the word of one of the gods of Egypt. Pharaoh was considered to be the human representative of the sun god, Ra.

Jochabed, Moses' mother, kept him hidden for three months, but she no doubt knew in her heart that this was only a temporary fix. Perhaps she hoped the edict would be withdrawn. Perhaps she hoped she could smuggle the baby away. Nevertheless, there would have been an increasing circle of those who were aware of a crying infant. Finally, when she was forced to put him in the river, she arranged a basket and set it in a place where Pharaoh's daughter was known to bathe. The Nile River had numerous side channels meandering through the reeds and as the basket was placed in the water, Moses' sister Miriam stood guard to watch over it (Exod. 2:4). This Hebrew word for basket here is the same one used in Genesis 6 when God commanded Noah to make an ark to rescue his family from the flood. Just as they were preserved through the catastrophic destruction of the flood, so also God's chosen deliver Moses was preserved from certain death in the waters of the Nile.

Pharaoh's daughter saw the basket, her servant woman brought it to her, and the child's cry captured her heart. She recognized the baby as one of the doomed Hebrew boys, but she took him to be her own son. That would mean rearing him right under the nose of the king! To be sure, the Pharaohs had an abundance of wives and children, and it may be that Moses escaped special notice since Pharaoh's daughter cleverly arranged to have his own mother nurse him. Having his cultural heritage firmly instilled by his mother, and then learning court protocol from years as the son of Pharaoh's daughter, prepared Moses for the dramatic role he would eventually play in leading God's people out of Egypt. That would be the greatest deliverance of all of Israel's history.

ZIPPORAH: MOSES' MIDIANITE WIFE

In the meantime, however, it seemed that the whole plan was seriously derailed. Moses killed an Egyptian. Word got out and Moses was on the run—to a place called Midian. That meant abruptly leaving the sumptuous court life and surviving as a semi-nomadic shepherd in the vast and barren wildernesses where the Midianite tribes roamed. He was content to stay with the family of a priest of Midian; it was a safe place far from those who might be trying to track him down. And he made a good first impression. The priest's daughters had been rudely treated by other shepherds as they tried to water their flocks, and Moses came to their rescue. Chances are the priest was slightly chagrined that he had seven daughters; no son is mentioned. Thus, he was delighted to give one of his daughters, Zipporah, to Moses, thereby gaining a son. At this point, Moses' Egyptian and Israelite identity was radically altered. Now, he was also related to a priest from Midian. Moses and Zipporah lived in tents, ranging across the Sinai wilderness to shepherd the flocks, and she bore him two sons.

Although we do not know much about Zipporah, one incident gives us a bit of insight into her wisdom. After God appeared to Moses at Mount Horeb and commissioned him to lead God's people to freedom, the small family headed back toward Egypt. We can only imagine how Zipporah felt about this prospect. Yes, she was the daughter of a priest, but a Midianite priest's life was different from an Egyptian's. Her life was consumed with tents, flocks, wells, and living on the move in the wilderness. It was rugged, but their nomadic existence spelled freedom. It must have been with a good deal of trepidation that she joined Moses on this venture back to Egypt. He had fled the court forty years earlier. How different that would be, if they even got into the court. Who knew whether the Israelites would welcome them—or not? What would Moses have to say to Pharaoh? Questions must have flooded her heart. She was no longer young. We cannot help but think of the courage of Sarah and Rebekah. All of these women were called to move into entirely new and unsettling situations.

En route back to Egypt, something very odd happened. In fact, it was so bizarre that Bible scholars are at a loss to explain it. In Exodus 4:24–26, we read that God confronted Moses and was about to kill him. We don't know why, and the details of the narrative are ambiguous. First, it is not certain who the "him" is that God threatened to kill. Was it Moses—or a son? He and Zipporah had two sons and one thing we do know. They had not circumcised them, as the covenant with Abraham required. When the first one was born, they named him Gershom which means "a stranger there," in a foreign land. Perhaps this name reflected Moses' own self-identity, or lack of it, at that point. From his perspective, he had utterly failed to bring deliverance to his people, even though he had tried to help them. Maybe he severed all traditional connections with his heritage in order to forget what seemed like an unredeemable failure. Or perhaps he wanted to circumcise the boy and Zipporah found it a barbaric custom and refused. We simply do not know. Because they named the second child Eliezer, meaning "my God is help," it seems that Moses was still profoundly aware of his relationship with God.

What the text does tell us is that it was Zipporah who knew what to do when God confronted them that dark evening. She was the one who promptly performed the circumcisions, even though her words in doing so seemed tinged with anger. What did she mean by saying Moses was a "bridegroom of blood"? And how did that relate to circumcision? Again, we just don't know. What we do know is that Moses sent Zipporah and the boys back to her father's tents until the ordeal in Egypt was over. After the triumphant crossing of the Sea of Reeds, they were reunited as her father brought Zipporah and her sons back to Moses. In fact, it seems that her whole clan joined themselves to the people of Israel when they heard the story of what God had done for his people.

When Moses took Zipporah as his wife, he was blessed with an exceptional woman. Even though they were from two distinct cultures, she seems to have understood and adopted his. She helped make Midian a haven for him, providing solace and restoration. At the same time, she was not afraid to confront him when his serious disregard for the covenant endangered them all. When she agreed to venture back to Egypt into the face of frightening unknowns, she demonstrated her courage as well as her commitment to Moses and his mission. And finally, because of Zipporah's faithfulness to Moses and his God, her father and extended family came under the wing of God's protecting grace.

GOD'S ROLE FOR RAHAB

After spending forty years wandering in the wilderness, God brought Israel to the edge of the Promised Land. From a safe position east of the Jordan River, Joshua sent spies across the river with instructions to pay special attention to Jericho. It was a strategic location on the front lines for anyone crossing into Canaan. Think of Joshua's concern to get this right. After all, he was filling the vacuum left by the death of Moses. And think of the king of Jericho's dismay when he heard reports and possibly saw evidence of the formidable number of people gathering to cross over into the land.

In the midst of these tense political developments, God used the Canaanite prostitute Rahab, who operated in the city of Jericho, to save the lives of the Israelite spies. What an unlikely candidate, we might think, for heroic action on behalf of the Israelites! And we might ask what the spies were doing in the establishment of a harlot. The truth is, however, that it would have been excellent cover. Lots of travelers probably visited there; the spies could mingle among them. Further, Rahab's location was eminently "convenient." Her house was built into the city wall, providing access without making a spectacle at the city gate.

This small detail is intriguing from another perspective. Cities in ancient Israel were generally surrounded by doubled walls that had living space in between the inside and outside stone walls. Those, like Rahab, who lived there were actually the first line of defense when the city was threatened. Clearly, these would be the lower classes of citizens, families and persons whose lives were considered "dispensable." In more contemporary terms, they were the human shield. Jumping ahead in the story, it was from that room in the wall that Rahab suspended the scarlet cord, visible to the first attackers when the Israelites stormed the city.

Even though the king of Jericho demanded that Rahab hand over the Israelite men, she hid them on her roof under stalks of flax and reported that the spies had left. Her reason? She had heard of God's

miraculous actions on behalf of Israel, from crossing the sea to defeating major kings on the east side of the Jordan River. The word had
spread and she feared the Lord more than she feared the king of Jericho.

She also made the Israelites vow that they would offer protection
and show kindness (*ḥesed*) to her and her family when they returned.
This word translated "kindness" is rich with meaning. It is best understood as loyal covenant love and generally refers to God's love and
great mercy to His people. Nonetheless, it also is faithful kindness and
mercy between people who are bound to one another in a treaty or
covenant. Rahab expected that these men would honor her kindness
to them. After all, she had defied the king and put herself in jeopardy
had she been discovered to have protected the Israelites.

But how would they know, in the messiness of the forthcoming
battle, whom to spare? They had no idea at this point how it would
unfold. The signal they arranged was that she would hang a scarlet cord
in the city wall window where she lived. She was to gather her extended
family there, and all who were inside would be spared. This is a striking reminder of the Passover celebration when the blood of the Passover
lamb marked on doorposts protected all those who were in their houses.
Indeed, Rahab and her family survived the dramatic siege of Jericho and
the subsequent complete destruction.

Rahab lived in Israel and went on to marry into the line of Judah,
the tribe from which the Messiah would come. How do we know that?
Centuries later, when Matthew recounted the genealogy of Jesus Christ
for his Jewish audience, he noted, "Salmon the father of Boaz by Rahab"
(Matt. 1:5). Also, both James and the author of Hebrews affirm Rahab's
faith and faithfulness. Not only did she hear and believe the reports about
the power of the God of Israel, she did what she could in her circumstances—and it was just the right thing. Neither James nor the author of
Hebrews hides her unsavory lifestyle. They label her "Rahab the prostitute," but it is clear that she was one whom God loved and redeemed *and*
called into active service.

God handed the city of Jericho over to the Israelites. They went on to take the land of Canaan and finally settled in the land promised to Abraham and his descendants just about six hundred years earlier. In the midst of it all, the Lord gave Rahab an important role in his plan. Unlikely? Impossible? Yes, in human terms. But God was in the business of keeping his covenant then, just as he is now.

FURTHER REFLECTION

Let's return to our opening reflections on the unwelcoming treatment outsiders often receive from the likes of us. Isn't it interesting that, with the exception of Potiphar's wife, the foreign women we've studied in this chapter—who no doubt would cause some raised eyebrows—were the ones who initially showed kindness to the Israelites, not the other way around? It's rather like Jesus' response to the question: "And who is my neighbor?" (Luke 10:29). Given the context, the question really is: "Whom am I supposed to love?" But Jesus turned it around, telling the familiar Good Samaritan parable. It was the Samaritan, despised and considered outside the bounds of Judaism, who demonstrated what love looked like. As I think of attitudes and perceptions entrenched in my own heart, I know I have a lot to learn.

Of course, here's the big question: Is there any warrant for us to follow the examples of Rahab or the midwives in Egypt? Should we ever consider lying to be the correct moral choice? God blessed the Egyptian midwives for their bold lie. The Israelites not only welcomed Rahab into their people; she was a major figure in the line of David. What is the common factor in these incidents? Consider the well-known description by Corrie Ten Boom in *The Hiding Place* of the contrast between her sister, who would not lie no matter what, and herself, who knew in her heart that lying was necessary to save a precious life. In God's most wonderful provision, the convictions of each were honored.

What is the "take-home" from all of this? First, it is *not* permission to deceive whenever the truth is inconvenient for us. The Scriptures are consistently clear, from Genesis to Revelation, that lying is detestable to God. These incidents do, however, provide a pattern for those uncommon and horrifying instances when human lives are in jeopardy. Then, intently seeking God's wisdom in prayer, it may be an option. But it ought not be an easy or first choice.

EIGHT

Deborah: a Leader in Israel

Deborah was one of Israel's major political and spiritual leaders during a time when God's people had spiraled down into increasing depths of wickedness and degradation. They had rejected the Lord and turned to the idols of the people around them. Sound familiar? In Israel's case, God punished them, which was completely in keeping with what he had promised in the covenant. If they were faithful, God would bless them with security and freedom from famine (Lev. 26:3–13). If, however, they were disobedient, death and destruction at the hands of enemies would be the result. God's purposes in this were not to be harsh and cruel. Instead, it was his intent to bring Israel to repentance, acknowledging he was their sovereign, loving God, while idols were empty, powerless, and entirely incapable of justice or mercy (Lev. 26:14–45).

JABIN, KING OF HAZOR, AND DEBORAH, JUDGE OF ISRAEL

It happened rather early in the period of the judges that God used a king named Jabin to oppress Israel for twenty years. Jabin was king of Hazor, the largest and most powerful of the Canaanite cities in the northern part of Israel. It was, for the sake of comparison, about twenty times larger than Jerusalem at that time. Jabin's military technology was significantly more advanced than anything Israel had; he had 900 iron chariots, probably the equivalent of holding the threat of nuclear power. In other words, when he started saber-rattling, the people living nearby would experience the ominous threat. God called Deborah right into the middle of that brewing conflict!

During that era, Israel was a collection of related tribes who often squabbled until they needed each other and even then, assistance was not always immediately forthcoming! The land where they had settled was small, but the rugged hill country meant they could be sufficiently removed to ignore problems if they did not want to "get involved." Deborah's location near Bethel was about fifty miles south of Jabin's military activity. We'll return to that in a moment.

From the narrative, we learn that all Israel came to Deborah in order to settle their disputes (Judg. 4:5). Her leadership was so effective that having to travel the length of the land did not deter people from seeking her wisdom and counsel. It is clear that she was a compelling presence. This is manifested in several ways. First, she is described as "the wife of Lappidoth" (Judg. 4:4) at the outset of the story. That may simply mean "married to a guy named Lappidoth," but there is a possibility it is a description of Deborah herself. The Hebrew word for "wife" is the same as the word for "woman" and a *lapid* is a "torch." Do you get the picture? Maybe, just maybe, this is saying she was a fiery woman, a dynamite personality! Second, when she told someone to do something, it was a good idea to follow her command. We will see that Barak, the man God and Deborah appointed as commander of Israel's armed forces, appeared when summoned. Finally, in addition to being a judge, Deborah was also a prophet, which meant that God used her to speak His word to His people.

BARAK'S ORDERS

In the face of the threat from Jabin, Deborah sent for Barak. He lived near the city of Hazor and thus felt the pressure of Jabin's forces. It would have taken him about two days to travel to Bethel, but he went—no questions asked. Deborah told him to prepare an army for battle with Sisera, the general of Jabin's army, and declared that Israel would be victorious. At this point, however, Barak balked. He said he would not go without her. From our human perspective, this makes a lot of sense. After all, he had lived in the area ravaged by Jabin's forces and knew what they could do. Deborah's command to muster 10,000 Israelite men really meant gathering an army of untrained soldiers. How would they function against well-trained operatives? Furthermore, Deborah was a known prophet and a strong and trusted leader, and Barak needed the confidence of her presence.

On the other hand, God's word to him through Deborah that he would be successful should have been sufficient. This was a matter of trust. Barak suffered from a lack of faith in God's power. In fact, he had put his trust in a *person* instead of in the promise of God, a temptation with which we are painfully familiar.

In a remarkable combination of rebuke and reassurance, Deborah told him she would accompany him, but he would not be remembered for winning the battle. Instead of his personally defeating Sisera, the general of the army of Hazor, that honor would go to a woman named Jael. A woman of all things! In that culture, where honor and shame were part of the very fabric of existence, this would have been devastating and humiliating.

THE BATTLE WITH SISERA

Deborah journeyed north with Barak. In fact, the biblical text says twice that she was with him (Judg. 4:9-10). That was just as she had promised. The Israelite forces gathered on Mt. Tabor overlooking the Jezreel Valley, a military arena for centuries. This was no doubt at Deborah's instruction. As leader, prophet, and judge of Israel, she would know strategic battle grounds and know how to use them. She knew that Sisera's iron chariots, well-suited for the broad valley, could do nothing against the steep slopes of Mt. Tabor. She also knew something else. At just the right time, Deborah uttered the command that sent the Israelites hurtling down the slopes.

When there are torrents of rain, the Jezreel Valley, drained by the Kishon River and its tributaries, turns into a sea of mud. When Barak's forces moved down the mountainside, the text says that the *Lord* defeated all of Sisera's chariots and army. The poetry in Judges 5 says, "[f]rom the heavens the stars fought, from their courses they fought against Sisera. The river Kishon swept them away . . . " (5:20-21). Sisera's superior military equipment—iron chariots—bogged down and all the enemy forces were destroyed as Israel pursued them. This victory was entirely God's doing, and Deborah was God's faithful prophet, giving the word to move into action.

JAEL: A VALIANT WOMAN

Sisera, the enemy general, left his chariot and ran for his life, deserting what was left of his army. He came exhausted to the tent of a woman named Jael, the wife of a man named Heber of the clan of Kenites. These people had managed to live on the boundary between allegiance to Israel and peaceful relations with the oppressive forces of Hazor.

Jael welcomed Sisera into her tent. She arranged a comfortable place to rest, assured him he had nothing to worry about, and put him to sleep with a drink of milk. She waited until he was fast asleep and then hammered a tent peg through his head—apparently without flinching. What a bold and gutsy woman! The poetry of Judges 5 is graphic: " . . . she struck Sisera; she crushed his head; she shattered and pierced his temple" (verse 26). A little later, Barak came by in hot pursuit of Sisera—and his own honor. Jael knew she had the prize he wanted. She showed him the dead body of Sisera, with the evidence of her own heroic act still in place.

THE SONG OF DEBORAH

While the prose narrative says nothing more about Deborah, we have one rich resource that gives us further glimpses into the character of this remarkable woman. "On that day, Deborah sang this song . . . " (Judg. 5:1). Although it does not come through in English, the structure of this Hebrew introduction indicates clearly that it was *Deborah* who was singing. Barak joined in. To sing was to teach and plant the recital of these events deeply in the hearts of the people. Here we see that one of Deborah's roles was national teacher! Singing was and is an excellent memory aid. Remember the song Moses taught the Israelites after they crossed the Sea of Reeds (Exod. 15:1–18). Once he composed it, Miriam also sang in order to teach the women (Exod. 15:21). Israel's national hymnbook, the Psalms, served the same purpose of reminding the people of God's faithfulness.

In this song, Deborah praised God for his mighty acts on behalf of Israel. She also recorded the valiant deeds of those who joined the fight against the oppressors, from noble tribesmen to Jael, and rebuked those who stayed behind, not getting involved. Deborah was not shy about mentioning her own role as "a mother in Israel" (Judg. 5:7) when the land had been desolated.

We don't know how long Deborah continued to serve as judge. We do read at the end of Judges 5 that the land had peace for forty years, which suggests a good long generation. In a world where wars erupted far too often, forty years of peace was truly a blessing.

FURTHER REFLECTIONS

We all know that trust in God is . . . well, it is absolutely foundational to our lives as children of our heavenly Father. And yet it seems so difficult to do. I don't know about you, but my life story seems to consist of one incident after another of being nervous, afraid, terrified at the prospects of all the things that I imagine could go wrong. I'm the Barak of this narrative. Somewhere in that web of fear, I lose the sense that my loving God and heavenly Father *is* able to work in this situation for good—both mine and the good of those I dearly love. After each imagined crisis is over, I emerge chastened with the reminder of how faithful and good God is. And then, the next time is a repeat performance of the same set of nerves and anxiety. It seems as if I have not learned even one thing about resting in the "everlasting arms." Have you been there?

How do we learn to trust? One important avenue—which we so often neglect—should be meditating on God's great and precious promises (2 Pet. 1:3-4). This is not a new insight; it's just another gentle reminder. We need to be prodded to memorize and sing of God's truth and experience the powerful sustenance that provides. This takes time; it means slowing down to consider his bountiful and unfailing goodness in the past, and his steadfast promises for the future. Then, instead of being untrained, we will be armed and ready.

A second avenue is listening to the people God has brought into our lives to give us encouragement, rebuke, and direction when we falter. We may not be Deborahs—yet—but a significant step in growing our courage and actively serving the Lord will involve enlisting those whom we trust to be faithful to speak the truth as we need to hear it.

NINE

Samson's Mother: Thinking Clearly

BIBLICAL TEXT: JUDGES 13–16

Another significant woman moved to the center of the biblical stage as the judges continued to lead Israel. Ironically, she is not even named, yet her faith and faithfulness outshone those of her husband and certainly her son. She is Samson's mother, always referred to as "Manoah's wife."

THE PATTERN IN THE BOOK OF JUDGES

The pattern that shaped the Israelites' story during the time of Deborah continued and intensified as they spiraled downward. It's a human pattern, it seems. We stumble along in our darkness, intent on satisfying our own wants. Individuals, communities, peoples, and nations fail to be obedient to what they know is right. One of God's ways of rescuing us from the ultimate consequences of our folly is to bring disasters of one kind or another to turn our attention back to him. Invariably, after such incidents—whether earthquakes, hurricanes, or something as horrifying as a terrorist attack—many more people are drawn to the church. We repent and humble ourselves, confessing our sins in prayer. God mercifully restores us and we vow to serve him faithfully, which we do, for a while. But then we head right back to the things we said we would never do again.

So it was toward the end of the period of Israel's judges. The people had sunk again to a low, low place and were worshiping the idols they thought would bring them security and prosperity. This time, God used the Philistines to turn Israel's attention back to the Source of their individual and national life and hope. The Philistines were a powerful people living on the coast of the Mediterranean Sea. They had international connections, were significantly more cosmopolitan than the hill country Israelites and, like the people of Hazor, they had advanced technology in the form of iron. A working comparison would be the continuous "city" from Boston to Washington, DC. Its population stands in stark contrast to folks who hail from the lovely and isolated Adirondack Mountains. And we will find that this "city" repeatedly offers temptations to those who are from more provincial backgrounds. That is exactly where Samson found himself.

AN ANGEL OF THE LORD VISITED SAMSON'S MOTHER: MANOAH'S WIFE

Samson's mother was married to a man named Manoah, who lived in one of the towns near the border with the Philistines. Even though we know *his* name and not that of his wife, it turns out that the angel of the Lord appeared first to *her,* not to Manoah (Judg.13:2–5). As the story continues, we may get an idea why that was so.

Like many of our previous characters, this woman was not able to have children. And also like many of them, she was privileged to receive a visit and special communication from the angel of the Lord, who represented the Lord himself. He announced that she would have a son and then he gave her very specific instructions—quite odd instructions if she did not know her Israelite heritage. She was not to drink wine or touch or eat anything unclean. If she did, that uncleanness would pass along to her son. Furthermore, he was not to cut his hair because he was called by God to be a Nazirite. A what?

UNDERSTANDING THE NAZIRITE VOW

We need to go back to the law God revealed through Moses at Mt. Sinai in order to understand what this was all about. In Numbers 6, we learn that God gave instructions regarding a special vow, called the Nazirite vow. Someone who would be a Nazirite was specifically set apart to accomplish God's purposes. Probably the closest parallel now would be God's call to join a monastery or a convent for the purpose of devoting one's entire life to service.

Both men and women could take the Nazirite vow upon themselves, for either their lifetime or just a limited period. Samson was set apart for a lifetime vow even before he was born. As this narrative tells us, called to be a Nazirite meant Samson would have to stay away from wine, not go near a dead body—which represented the most serious kind of uncleanness, and not cut his hair. The long hair was the specific sign that the person was called and set apart by God.

In Samson's case, God's purpose was to deliver Israel from the Philistines, who were making life utterly miserable for them. Notice, by the way, that God determined to use the Philistines to bring chastisement on his wayward children, but that did not mean the Philistines got off scot-free. They were ripe for their own judgment.

MANOAH RECEIVED THE REPORT FROM HIS WIFE

We don't know where Manoah's wife was when the angel of the Lord spoke to her. Later on, when the angel returned the second time, she was out in the field, most likely at work. Perhaps that was true the first time as well. We do know that she went to Manoah and repeated the message she had received. She seems to have been uncertain as to just who had appeared to her. She called him a man of God, the title usually given to a prophet, but also called him the angel of God. She was impressed with his appearance as well as his message, and called him "awesome" as she described him. And by the way, "awesome" does not mean "oh, really cool," as it is currently used. Properly understood, this word means someone or something that inspires heart-stopping reverence, if not outright terror.

Manoah's wife faithfully represented the message to him, carefully including the details about what not to do and the fact that their son would be a Nazirite. Possibly not satisfied that his wife could convey the proper information, Manoah seems to have wanted to hear the specific requirements for himself. He prayed, asking God to send the person back again to teach them how to bring up the child. The angel of the Lord appeared to the woman again and she ran to tell Manoah. He followed her out to the field where he found the man and asked if he was the same person who addressed his wife previously. When the angel of the Lord said "I am," Manoah then inquired about the child's future mission. No doubt he had in mind the weight of the Nazirite vow.

The angel did not respond to that query, but he did answer Manoah's question about how they were to rear the child. What is downright amusing is that the angel of God commanded exactly the same things he had said before, no additional details, just a reassuring confirmation for Manoah. Interestingly, he placed the entire responsibility for observing the restrictions on the woman. Given Samson's subsequent rebellion against every aspect of the vow, we have to wonder how his mother communicated to him his identity as a Nazirite. Why did he come to view the vow as simply a bothersome set of restrictions? Samson seems to have rejected everything that defined him as an Israelite. What a tangled web of solemn commands, good intentions, and deliberate disobedience, all securely under God's sovereign design!

THE IDENTITY OF THE ANGELIC VISITOR

Following his brief exchange with the angel, Manoah wanted to prepare an offering. Maybe it was a polite religious gesture; maybe it was out of true fear and awe. He also asked the name of the angel. The angel answered and said that his name was "too wonderful," which is the same Hebrew word as we read in Isaiah 9:6, "For unto us a child is born, unto us a son is given, and His Name shall be called *Wonderful* Counselor, Mighty God, Everlasting Father, Prince of Peace . . . "

When the sacrificial animal was ready, the angel himself disappeared in the flame rising above the altar. Manoah and his wife fell on their faces, knowing they had been in the presence of the angel of the Lord and had even *looked* at God. Manoah was terrified and said "We shall surely die!" His wife, a more logical and careful thinker, said, "If the Lord had meant to kill us, He would not have accepted a burnt offering and a grain offering from our hands, nor shown us all these things, or now told us this" (Judg. 13:23).

SAMSON REJECTED HIS PARENTS, HIS PEOPLE, HIS VOW

Manoah's wife bore a son and they named him Samson. As he grew up, the Spirit of the Lord was at work in him, but there were lots of other pressures and emotions as well, and Samson succumbed to temptation with distressing ease. No doubt his mother's heart was deeply wounded as he broke his Nazirite vow and treated his parents with obvious contempt. He seemed to despise their rigid traditions. What was the point of a vow that he did not care about? Why did they impose this whole set of restrictions on him?

All Samson's life, he was attracted to Philistine women. The first time around, he demanded that his parents arrange the wedding. The young woman was from a Philistine town just down the valley from where Samson lived. It seems that the temptations, and particularly the sexual temptations, of the looser and more cosmopolitan culture, were just too alluring for Samson.

Think of his parents' dismay! How could they possibly arrange a wedding with a family that was one of the enemy? What would the neighbors say? We get just a tiny picture of their extreme discomfort from one verse in the story: "His father and mother replied, 'Isn't there an acceptable woman among your relatives or among all our people? Must you go to the uncircumcised Philistines to get a wife?'" (Judg. 14:3). It was worse than Romeo and Juliet or its modern counterpart, *West Side Story*! And then the next verse indicates something remarkable. His parents did not know this was from the Lord, whose plan it was to confront the Philistines right from the start. In other words, even Samson's outright disobedience and contemptuous demands were not outside God's plan. In fact, this was the beginning of a series of challenges to Philistine dominance. Nevertheless, we can imagine the heartache and shame for Samson's mother as one wretched incident in his life followed another.

Samson's first wife and her father were killed by Philistines in response to Samson's attack on their grain fields. As he continued on his reckless way, he ranged far into Philistine territory along the Mediterranean coast, at one point consorting with a prostitute from Gaza, one of the major Philistine cities. Each of Samson's actions prompted an angry and violent response from the more powerful Philistine people who had persistently pressed into the heartland of the Israelite hill country. No doubt his mother saw how Samson's vengeful spirit kept that cycle of destructive violence going (Judg. 15). When her son was finally caught and imprisoned, she probably heard the story of Delilah. It seems that maybe, just maybe, Samson had been trying to return home in his own faltering way.

Delilah lived in the same general area as Samson's first wife—just down the valley from the tribal inheritance of Dan from which Samson hailed. Nevertheless, he did not make it home. Samson's mother would hear of his complete humiliation in the lap of this woman. She would know that with his hair cut, the Nazirite vow was completely broken. And that would shatter whatever hope she had left. How she must have struggled to wrap her mind around this! Her boy had despised everything she and Manoah had so carefully done to enable Samson to keep his lifelong vow. How on earth was this rebellious son set apart to God? What purposes did she see fulfilled in the string of violent attacks and sordid affairs?

THE DEATH OF SAMSON

No doubt the Israelites felt Samson's previous triumphs were short-lived when the Philistines had him bound in chains in Gaza. Certainly, the Philistines were bragging: "Our god has delivered our enemy into our hands, the one who laid waste our land and multiplied our slain" (Judg. 16:24). And then with one last act, still in the spirit of vengeance, Samson brought down the entire temple of Dagon on their heads. He knew he would die in the process. His only care was to make a final devastating swipe in revenge for their having blinded him (Judg. 16:28–30).

When his family came to retrieve his body and take it home for burial—the final event in Samson's tragic life—Scripture mentions his brothers and his father's whole family, but not his mother (Judg. 16:31). We can only guess at the reasons for this omission. It may simply be that the men of the family would be expected to do the heavy work of transporting a coffin. Perhaps the cultural prominence of men shapes this part of this narrative as well. Or it may be that this narrative silence is the only possible representation of a mother's response to such a violent death—the last in a long series of vicious retaliations.

FURTHER REFLECTIONS

As Samson's mother relived each sordid incident in her son's life, she must have questioned over and over again how she had failed so miserably in the charge given to her by the angel of the Lord. Had she imposed restrictions in ways that pushed him into rebellion? We can imagine her sense of unending guilt and self-recrimination in those years when he was wandering far away from his people and his God.

What does this story say to mothers whose children have caused them great anguish?

Above all, there is comfort in knowing that God used even the cruel rejection of everything Samson's mother stood for and tried to teach him. In fact, in ways that seem unfathomable to us, Samson's vengeful spirit and weakness for women were the very means God used to break the Philistines' iron hold on Israel at that time. In the same way, none of the shattered pieces of our lives or our children's lives are beyond God's power to redeem and use them. And Jesus still says, "Come unto Me all you who are weary and heavy-laden and I will give you rest" (Matt. 11:28). He is in the business of restoring and mending the torn places in our hearts.

One more question: How do we uphold what we know to be God's design for our children when the entire surrounding culture beckons them to pursue fun, instant gratification, and intense excitement? I do not have easy answers here. In fact, my readers will do much better than I, but as I think back over families whose children have navigated those treacherous waters safely, I have observed several patterns that revolve around nurturing joy and gratitude. The Apostle Paul had it right—"Be joyful always; pray continually; give thanks in all circumstances, for this is God's will for you in Christ Jesus" (1 Thess. 5:16–18). Oh yes, there are many other godly characteristics as well, but this combination is a specific antidote to the allure from "outside." Neither can be artificially manufactured; it is our task to pray earnestly for God's Spirit to fill us daily—in fact, moment by moment.

Let us pray that our lives will be vibrant with joy in one another, joy in beauty, even joy in facing challenges. Jesus promises that his coming means "life to the full" (John 10:10). Within that environment, the empty shells that pass as excitement and fun are stripped bare of their superficial appeal. And then let us covenant to give thanks in *all* things.

TEN

Ruth and Naomi:
Unfailing Covenant Love

BIBLICAL TEXTS: BOOK OF RUTH

A number of years ago, I was asked whether anything in the book of Ruth really speaks to today's Christian woman. At the time, I was presenting a day-long women's seminar focused entirely on Ruth, so I thought, "There had better be!" One of the major issues we talked about that day was the nature of God as he cares for women who have lost everything.

Just as we discovered in our earlier studies, we will see here that God provides. If we learn nothing else from our entire study of women in the Bible, let us learn that God is the hero of your story and mine. He is the hero because, no matter how bad things are, heroes make things come out right in the end. God does just that. It is true that the end usually feels a long way from the dismal present. And it is much easier to talk about trust and obedience than to trust and obey. Nevertheless, we must pray for the assurance that with God, nothing is impossible. We need also to remember that he is our ruler and, as such, he rules our hearts as well as our circumstances.

Israel: the Testing Ground of Faith

This would be true for Ruth and Naomi; at the opening of the book, their circumstances were grim. As we consider their story, it is important to step back just a bit in order to understand what was happening to the people of Israel at this time. As we have already seen, theirs was a history of recurring lack of trust, along with disobedience. Once they settled in the land, they continued to rebel against the God who had rescued them from bondage in Egypt and provided daily for their needs in the wilderness. They turned to idols and false gods.

Whenever the people set out on their own self-serving paths, God used something that would turn their hearts back to him. Sometimes it was foreign invaders and war. The Philistines we encountered in the Samson narrative were a prime example. Sometimes it was famine in the land which was the result of lack of rain. The crops died; the animals and people also died from hunger and thirst (Deut. 11:10–17). In our day, seeing journalistic photos of hollow-eyed skeletons walking miles to escape the ravages of famine and war may help us understand why our first characters in Ruth tried to leave an area of famine.

Famine in Bethlehem

So it was during the period of Israel's judges. Bethlehem, which we already recognized as the town of David, suffered a severe famine. In a touch of irony, the name Bethlehem means "house of bread," yet there was none. The family of a man named Elimelech had to leave their land near Bethlehem. They crossed the Dead Sea to the east of Israel and settled in Moab. If you have a map handy in your Bible, take a look at these locations. The areas around the Dead Sea are dry and barren, so the journey to Moab would not have been easy. It may be that Moab itself had not suffered from the lack of rainfall to the extent that Israel did. In any case, it was viewed as a haven from the famine even though it was foreign and sometimes not very hospitable territory.

NAOMI: WIFE OF ELIMELECH

Elimelech's wife was named Naomi. The couple had two sons. When the boys were old enough to marry, they both took wives from among the Moabite people. One was Ruth; the other was Orpah. In other words, these folks really settled into their Moabite surroundings.

Naomi's name is related to a Hebrew word meaning "delightful" or "pleasant." Hebrew names have significance and initially, Naomi's name seems to have fit both her circumstances and her personality. From later details in the story we see that she was married into a family that had some sort of estate in the area of Bethlehem. Her husband's name, Elimelech, means "my God is King," suggesting his family's allegiance to the covenant God of Israel.

DEATH OF ELIMELECH AND THE TWO SONS

Although they had escaped the famine in Judah, the men of the family did not escape death. First, Elimelech died, leaving Naomi a widow. Then, after about ten years, her two sons also died. Her entire family was gone. Adding to her grief and insecurity was the fact that she was an Israelite woman in a foreign land. Both her widowed daughters-in-law had family to whom they might return; she had no one. Naomi's bitterness and sorrow were overwhelming. The family's estate in Bethlehem was depleted. In moving to Moab, she had lost prospects for "good Israelite women" for her sons, and then her husband and two sons were taken away. Given the social and economic structure, a woman without father, husband, or sons was destined to starvation; no one would care for her. Here were three widows together!

NAOMI'S RETURN TO BETHLEHEM

At this point, Naomi heard that the famine in Bethlehem was over, and she determined to go home. It was a risky move, but what else could she do? Her decision, however, put Ruth and Orpah in a difficult position. Would they go with her and live as strangers and aliens in Israel? Or would they leave their mother-in-law to travel alone? As a widow, she most likely set out with very little in terms of provisions, only the hope that someone would take pity on her when she arrived back home. This reminds us of the scene with Hagar who set out alone in spite of the dangers for poor women, left on their own.

Death and utter desolation led Naomi to start her sojourn back to Bethlehem at the beginning of the barley harvest. The timing was significant. Barley would eventually be the source of her daily food.

ORPAH AND RUTH'S CHOICES

Both Orpah and Ruth travelled part way with Naomi. Knowing, however, how difficult their lives would be in Bethlehem as foreigners, she urged them to return to their mothers' homes, to their people, and to their gods. She wanted to spare her daughters-in-law the lonely, widowed existence that would surely be their lot in Bethlehem. She certainly recognized her own inability to provide her daughters-in-law with husbands, and they would stand little chance of finding Israelite men who would marry them. Maybe she was also embarrassed at bringing *two* Moabite women to what was left of her Bethlehem home. There would have been prejudice, and she may have been afraid of what would happen to them in Israelite culture as Moabite women. No doubt she was aware of Deuteronomy 23:3 which said that to the tenth generation, a Moabite could not enter the congregation of Israel. In other words, humanly speaking, it would have been disastrous to have these three widows living together.

We cannot help but notice Naomi's desire and willingness to provide for Ruth and Orpah. She was willing to sacrifice her own comfort and security on the journey for them. The relationship they shared was strong, with mutual bonds built on their love for each other.

After some urging, Orpah did turn back weeping, but Ruth clung to Naomi. Something about Naomi, even in these very difficult circumstances, bound Ruth to her. Perhaps it was her love, her faith, her strength of character that Ruth found compelling. Perhaps it was her utter honesty. Ruth's deep love for Naomi burst forth in unforgettable words. "Please do not make me leave you. Where you go, I will go and where you stay I will stay. Your people will be my people and your God will be my God. Where you die, I will die and there I will be buried" (Ruth 1:16-17). Ruth pledged to stay with Naomi to the end of her life.

As an aside, I've often wondered what happened to Orpah. In choosing to return to her Moabite family, she did opt for some kind of security. Do you suppose she had absorbed enough about Naomi's God that she became, in essence, a missionary to Moab? It is a comforting prospect.

NAOMI AND RUTH ARRIVED IN BETHLEHEM

Naomi and Ruth continued on together, bravely making their way by themselves through the dry land, east of Bethlehem, and up the rugged ascent to the town. Their arrival had the whole town talking. "Could this be Naomi?" She had been gone more than ten years, and life had not been kind to her. She was worn and weary. Both Elimelech *and* her sons were gone.

Now there was a young foreign woman with her, and Naomi's response to her former neighbors was painfully honest. It was God Almighty, she said, who had made her life so bitter, who had emptied her of everything worth caring about (Ruth 1:20-21). We might wonder how her words affected Ruth, who was so faithfully and lovingly accompanying her, yet received no acknowledgement.

Naomi was not silent about her feelings that God had abandoned her. Hers was the prospect of a lonely, difficult, marginal life. For a time, it seems that she could not see the great gift God had given her in Ruth's devotion.

NAOMI'S HONEST BITTERNESS

Naomi knew and *said* that the hand of God was against her. It was this knowledge that made her life seem so very bitter. Her God was her enemy; that is not something that is easily said or heard. In fact, it means the very foundations of our faith are shaking and in danger of toppling. And yet, such expression is honest, and God invites us to pour out the deepest anguish of our hearts. Naomi sounds very much like Job—who put the blame for his difficult circumstances squarely on God (Job 16:7–9, 11–14; 19:21; 30:18–23) and was not rebuked for doing so. In Naomi's case, perhaps she questioned whether earlier decisions to leave Judah or allow her sons to marry Moabite women were in disobedience to God's commands. Was she being punished? What might have been the reasons for the multiple disasters in her life?

As she responded to the incredulous question posed by the women of Bethlehem, Naomi focused on the contrast between her previous name and estate ("pleasant") and her current bitter circumstances. "Don't call me Naomi,' she told them. 'Call me Mara, because the Almighty has made my life very bitter. I went away full, but the LORD has brought me back empty. Why call me Naomi? The LORD has afflicted me; the Almighty has brought misfortune upon me" (Ruth 1:20-21). Naomi did have a profound sense of God's complete control of all circumstances, both good and ill. In God's perfect timing, her emptiness was perhaps what she needed most. It was only then that she was able to see the true, self-giving love Ruth was showing to her. Naomi had depended on her own ability to make things work as they should. Now, she was learning a tough lesson: she would need to accept help.

Gleaning in the Fields

Naomi and Ruth settled in Bethlehem at the time of the barley harvest, which was early spring. Because the two widows were reduced to complete poverty, Ruth went into the fields to glean behind those who were harvesting the grain. The Law of Moses provided gleaning as one of the ways to care for the poor and destitute. Every field owner was to command his workers not to pick up all the stalks of grain they had cut. Instead, they were to leave them for those who had the strength and energy to gather them. In an agriculturally based economy, this provision would be sufficient to meet the needs of those who had no land or means of producing their own food. In God's infinite wisdom, this provision kept the wealthy from being tight-fisted and also allowed the poor the dignity of working for their sustenance. At the same time, it *was* hard labor!

BOAZ: A TRULY GOOD MAN

In Ruth's case, God also demonstrated his protection by having her glean in the field of Boaz. A literal translation says "it happened a happening" that Ruth was working in a field belonging to Boaz, a relative of Elimelech and a good man (Ruth 2:1–3). That's the author's way of indicating that from the human perspective it seemed mere happenstance, but God's hand was at work.

Ruth worked hard all day with very little rest, even though it sounds as if she may not have fully understood the process. Later on in the day, Boaz told his field workers not to shame her if she did not do it quite right. She was taking some barley from the gathered grain rather than from the loose stalks lying on the ground (which was the proper way of gleaning). In fact, Boaz commanded his workers to leave extra for her.

Boaz took note right away that Ruth was in his field, and asked who she was. He found out that she was the young foreign woman who had come back with Naomi, and he told her to stay with his young women workers so she would be protected. Boaz seemed to know that an outsider such as Ruth might not be treated properly. He was concerned for her welfare and safety, and told the young men not to touch her. He was also concerned that she had enough water in the heat of the day and extra food during the meal time.

Ruth was overwhelmed by his kindness and asked why he was so good to her. Boaz's answer gives us a full picture of Ruth's faithfulness to keep her promise to Naomi. He had heard of Ruth's goodness, that she had left her own people and come as a foreigner to Bethlehem in order not to leave Naomi alone. Boaz pronounced a blessing on Ruth in the name of the Lord God of Israel, under whose wings she had come to take refuge. It was a beautiful picture of God's protection over all of them.

Ruth threshed her barley at the end of the day and went home that evening with a good amount to give to Naomi because Boaz had added to it. Naomi asked where she had worked. Ruth told her it was Boaz's field, and Naomi blessed him and told Ruth to stay in his fields for the remainder of the barley and wheat harvests. This she did, faithfully providing for Naomi.

Naomi's Plans for the Future

Although the story does not specifically say so, we might guess that Naomi had a conversation with Boaz about Ruth. She would know Boaz through the family connection. She did say that he was a kinsman-redeemer. That meant, as a close relative (kinsman), he was to buy back (redeem) the land of Elimelech to keep it in the family. When the famine struck Bethlehem some fifteen years before, Elimelech was unable to support his family because the crops of the land failed. Thus, they left. It seems that Naomi had returned to the land, but did not have the means to work it. It had to be sold to the nearest of kin to keep the land in the clan. In the Law of Moses (Lev. 25:25), there is provision made for buying back the land which has already been sold to someone else. Here the circumstances seem to have been a bit different.

Imagine Naomi as self-appointed matchmaker. In the next scene in the story, she told Ruth that she knew Boaz would be at the threshing floor that night. She suggested that Ruth put on her best clothes and go down to the threshing floor. She was to wait until the celebrations died down, and then go lie at the feet of Boaz! Naomi closed her instructions with, "He will tell you what to do," which suggests she and Boaz had already talked about it. This was not a mission for a prim and shy woman, by the way. The festivities at the threshing floor were quite a party. Boaz may well have been there as a mature presence to keep more youthful spirits under control.

BOAZ AS KINSMAN-REDEEMER

At the threshing floor that night, Boaz did indeed wake up to find Ruth lying at his feet! When he asked who this was, Ruth responded by asking him to spread the corner of his garment over her because he was a kinsman-redeemer. The expression "corner of the garment" sounds like what Boaz said to Ruth when he blessed her. He had asked that the God of Israel, under whose wings she had come to take refuge, would help her. It was a declaration of protection. Now Ruth turned it back to him.

Boaz promised Ruth that he would take up the business and legal aspects of the kinsman-redeemer role the next morning. She stayed at his feet all night, perhaps because stumbling through the crowd at that time would be dangerous. She left early and Boaz told her *not* to say that a *woman* had come to the threshing floor. It seems that she had crossed a boundary into men's territory that night, making her actions all that much more adventurous. When she left, Boaz gave her six measures of barley. She took them back to Naomi, along with a report of the evening's events.

Boaz praised Ruth for not pursuing other younger men. This implies that she had deliberately chosen to provide continuation of family name and property *for Naomi* by marriage within the extended family instead of finding someone younger who may have been more to her liking. Although that was expected behavior then, even though it goes against *our* ideals of love and marriage, it still was significant enough that Boaz commended her.

The next morning, Boaz was faithful to his word. He went to the town gate, which served rather like a combination of court and market. There he met one other man, who was a closer relative than he, and told him Naomi had a piece of land to sell that formerly belonged to Elimelech. At first the man agreed to redeem the land by purchasing it from Naomi, but then Boaz added a detail. The land, he said, also belonged to Ruth since Elimelech's sons would have inherited it. In order to maintain the family *name* along with the property, the kinsman-redeemer would also have to marry Ruth. This made the picture a bit different for him because children born to him and Ruth would mean less inheritance for his own sons. Thus, he told Boaz to buy the field and marked the transfer of his redeemer role to Boaz by removing his sandal. That was the custom.

The upshot of all this was that Boaz acquired the property and took Ruth as his wife. That meant she and Naomi would no longer be helpless, vulnerable widows. The elders of the town witnessed the bargain and pronounced a blessing on Ruth, that she be like Leah and Rachel, who together built up the house of Israel. Coming from Israelites, this was a very significant blessing and sign of acceptance. It was especially remarkable because their tradition said that Moabites, which Ruth was, could not join the congregation of Israel up to the tenth generation. There were long-standing reasons for this prohibition (Deut. 23:1–6), and it would have made them wary of Moabites coming into Israel. It is important to realize, however, that this did *not* forbid marrying Moabite women.

RUTH'S SON AND DESCENDANTS

Ruth gave birth to a son whom the women of Bethlehem declared was *another* kinsman-redeemer for Naomi. They named him Obed, and he was actually adopted as Naomi's own child in order to carry on the family line of Elimelech. While we might think of this as a heart-wrenching loss for Ruth, the extended family most likely all lived together, and their mutual care enriched all of their lives. The women blessed Ruth for her faithfulness and love for Naomi.

Obed was the father of Jesse, who was the father of David. While genealogies generally cause our eyes to glaze over, they emphasize the continuity of God's purposes through the ages. In Judaism, genealogies were extremely important to establish an individual's identity. They indicate that the process of history is not random; the people who are named are part of God's plan. These few names—Boaz, Obed, and Jesse—are part of the much longer genealogy in Matthew 1 where we read the lineage of Jesus Christ. Even more striking, Ruth's name is mentioned there as well. Ruth, the foreigner and outsider, is one of four significant women in Jesus' family line. And Jesus is the ultimate Kinsman-Redeemer, buying us back from bondage to sin and guilt, and providing relief from famine of the soul.

FURTHER REFLECTIONS

What lessons might we learn from this story? Shining through is Ruth's deep, abiding love for Naomi and her desire to serve her, apparently without any expectations of return. Ruth was willing to sacrifice for Naomi's well-being in spite of personal cost. With a small amount of imagination, we can guess that Ruth's own circumstances were painful in the extreme—a young widow, separated from family for the rest of her life, lonely—and yet she resolutely moved ahead and did so with a tender and sensitive heart, declaring her allegiance to Naomi's people and God. Her venture into the fields meant back-breaking labor to provide the barest necessities of food. Most of Ruth's choices involved significant risk, but they are recorded without any allusion to her agonizing over them. She simply did what she knew to be right.

Also, Ruth had an inspired ability to know when to obey Naomi! Both her choice of "disobedience" in not returning to her home land, and then of obedience in visiting Boaz by night, go against our "common sense." In the latter case, it may be that she knew Boaz and Naomi had been negotiating, and she knew the local customs in which the scheme as outlined was acceptable. Nevertheless, she was stepping into a risky situation—going out at dusk dressed to the nines, sneaking round the threshing floor, hiding out between the stalks of grain, tiptoeing up to Boaz, uncovering his feet (waiting for a yell), lying down, and then anticipating his reaction.

We must not ignore lessons from Naomi. How do *we* respond to the "heavy hand" of God? Is it with honesty? That was Naomi's reaction. She had a full sense of God's sovereign hand in her life and spoke with candor about it. At that utterly low point, she had come to the end of her own resources; she had to relinquish her self-sufficiency and lean on the strength of her young daughter-in-law. Surely that was not easy for Naomi, but it was precisely what she needed. How difficult it is for us to give up the control of all of our circumstances to God! How humbling it is to accept the love and help of others! How often we fume in our bitterness without seeing the gentle and good people God has graciously given to us to help bear our circumstances!

Clearly, something did bring Naomi out of her despair. I would suggest that Ruth's steadfastness, which is alluded to several times by Boaz, was a major part of that. Furthermore, Boaz's kindness was a living demonstration to Naomi that God had not forgotten her. It may be that she had no hope of bridging the cultural barrier for Ruth, but Boaz's actions indicated that it might become a possibility. With her faith rekindled, she took action. Her fear for herself and for Ruth changed to hope. All of the characters in the story were faithful to God and his people. Each offers a powerful illustration of promises made and promises kept.

Ruth lived in a dark age—not so different from the circumstances in which God's people repeatedly find themselves today. Her story is like a beacon, piercing the gloom of disobedience and idolatry that characterized Israel at that time. Ruth wholeheartedly joined those who were bound to God in covenant love. What's more, as a recipient of God's unfailing lovingkindness, Ruth's life was a reflection of that same generous love. May it be so with us!

ELEVEN

Hannah: Giving Back to God

BIBLICAL TEXTS: I SAMUEL 1–3

The theme of the Nazirite vow connects the story of Samson's mother with that of Samuel's mother, Hannah. God intended both of these men to serve him, and their mothers played an important part in their preparation. The way these women received this responsibility, however, was vastly different. It was God who had set apart Samson before he was born. On the other hand, Hannah promised God that if he would grant her heart's desire—a son—she would dedicate him to the Lord as a Nazirite.

INTRODUCING HANNAH

Like Sarah, Rebekah, Rachel, and Manoah's wife, Hannah was unable to have children. She shared the grief and longing that were steady undercurrents in the lives of these women before her. Each year she would go, along with her husband and his second wife, to Shiloh where they would worship the Lord God of Israel. Elkanah was her husband's name. He deeply loved Hannah, and gave her special double portions of the sacrificial meal when they went to Shiloh.

Elkanah's other wife, Peninah, had sons and daughters. She also had a major chip on her shoulder because Hannah was the more beloved wife. She was mocking and cruel, especially at the time of the annual journey to worship at Shiloh, when Elkanah's devotion to Hannah was even more obvious. We have seen this theme before. Competition and jealousy create bitter divisions in family circles. And we have to wonder if Elkanah was any help to Hannah when he told her to cheer up; she had him even though she had no children (1 Sam. 1:8)!

HANNAH'S VOW

One year when they were at Shiloh, Hannah was weeping bitterly and praying to God at the same time. It is clear that Hannah knew God. She called him Lord of Hosts, and she made a vow. When we read in the Old Testament about making vows, we must set aside the casual way our culture uses the word vow. The most telling examples are marriage vows, which we see broken far too often. In the Old Testament world, making vows was a serious matter. Breaking them was even more serious and carried severe consequences.

Hannah chose the most stringent vow, one that included a visible sign. She promised God that if he would give her a son, a razor would not be used on his head all the days of his life. Long hair was the sign of the Nazirite vow. It signified that her son would be set apart to serve the Lord all his life. Hannah also called herself God's servant; and this fits the content of her prayer and her remarkable vow (1 Sam. 1:11). What she wanted more than anything was a son and here she was, ready and willing to give that son back to the Lord. Hannah fully recognized *whose* son Samuel would be. She promised to give back to God what she asked God to give to her.

ELI AT THE TABERNACLE

Eli, the priest, was sitting near the entrance of the tabernacle. He saw Hannah's lips moving but did not hear anything. He was certain she had been drinking too much wine and he rebuked her. Imagine a somewhat suspicious head usher in church, eyeing a young person whose posture and movements might be just a bit too dramatic for the traditional community, and wondering how best to corral this individual before she distracts the entire congregation from the sermon!

Hannah responded by telling Eli she was in deep sorrow and had been praying to God. She said she was pouring out her heart to the Lord. In the depths of her grief, Hannah found the place to talk to God. She wept and spoke of all that troubled her. Eli had the good sense to bless Hannah as he sent her on her way, asking that the God of Israel would grant her request. Hannah's despair was lifted. The next morning after worshipping the Lord, she returned home with Elkanah, Peninah, and Peninah's children.

HANNAH KEPT HER VOW

In due time, Hannah became pregnant and bore a son. She named him Samuel, acknowledging that God had heard her prayer. Hannah was bold to ask God, but her request was not without cost. She made a vow with profound implications for her own longings and desires. God heard her prayer and answered. With God nothing is impossible.

And Hannah kept her vow. She nursed Samuel at home and when he was weaned, she took him—along with a bull, a measure of flour, and wine for the sacrifice—and went to Shiloh. Samuel was very young, but Hannah was intent on keeping her promise to the Lord. After they had slaughtered the bull, Hannah told Eli that God had answered her prayer for a son, and she was now giving him back to the Lord for his whole life. As she did so, she had no idea how significant Samuel would be in the history of God's people. She just knew the importance of being faithful—and she was.

A bull, by the way, was not just a large and rough animal. It was the most valuable and expensive offering that could be made. It was also one of the prescribed offerings when priests began their service (Lev. 8). Not only was Samuel being dedicated to God's service at the tabernacle; although his mother did not know it, he would eventually become a priest in place of Eli and his sons. There were sobering reasons for that; we will look at them later.

HANNAH'S SONG

Hannah *sang* even as she gave her only son back to the Lord and left him at Shiloh with Eli. It was not a lament; no, it was a song of joy. She knew without a shadow of a doubt into whose care she was committing her son. In fact, her song would be echoed centuries later, when Mary rejoiced at being chosen as the mother of Jesus.

> My heart rejoices in the LORD; in the LORD my horn is
> lifted high.
> My mouth boasts over my enemies, for I delight in your
> deliverance.
> There is no one holy like the LORD; there is no one besides you;
> There is no Rock like our God.
> Do not keep talking so proudly or let your mouth speak
> such arrogance,
> For the LORD is a God who knows, and by him deeds are
> weighed.
> The bows of the warriors are broken,
> but those who stumbled are armed with strength.
> Those who were full hire themselves out for food,
> but those who were hungry hunger no more.
> She who was barren has borne seven children,
> but she who has had many sons pines away.
> The LORD brings death and makes alive;
> he brings down to the grave and raises up.
> The LORD sends poverty and wealth; he humbles and he exalts.
> He raises the poor from the dust and lifts the needy from the
> ash heap;

he sets them with princes and has them inherit a throne
   of honor.
For the foundations of the earth are the LORD's;
upon them he has set the world.
He will guard the feet of his saints, but the wicked will be
   silenced in darkness.
It is not by strength that one prevails;
those who oppose the LORD will be shattered.
He will thunder against them from heaven;
the LORD will judge the ends of the earth.
He will give strength to his king and exalt the horn of
   his anointed (1 Sam. 2:1–10).

Once we study these lines thoughtfully, it becomes a bit clearer as to how Hannah was able to entrust her dear son to the Lord. She may not have thought much of the minister (Eli); his reputation as a poor father was undoubtedly common knowledge. It was not just a matter of being "the priest's kids" and getting into some minor rebellious scrapes. His sons were wicked and blasphemous. While Eli rebuked them, he did nothing to stop their sacrilegious activities (1 Sam. 2:12–25). Nevertheless, Hannah knew God was holy and just; she knew God had everything and everyone firmly in his powerful hands—and that is what counted.

GOD'S FAITHFUL RESPONSE TO HANNAH'S DEVOTION

When Hannah consecrated her firstborn wholeheartedly to the Lord, Eli blessed her and requested from God that she have more children. That prayer was also answered; Hannah had three more sons and two daughters. Her willingness to give to God what was already his meant further great blessings for her.

As time passed, Hannah came to Shiloh every year to bring a robe for Samuel as he grew. We have to wonder what their yearly visits were like. She was no doubt very proud of her boy, and overjoyed to see his increasing wisdom and maturity. We learn that he "continued to grow in stature and in favor with the LORD and with men" (1 Sam. 2:26). Hannah would see that and give thanks to God. Even though she may have viewed with suspicion those women who served at the entrance to the Tabernacle (1 Sam. 2:22), she had learned to trust that God is faithful. God had given her Samuel, and she knew beyond a shadow of a doubt that he would protect Samuel and prepare him for service. That was the essence of her Nazirite vow from the very beginning and it was sufficient to give her heart rest, even as she left each year on the long journey home.

Samuel grew up to become a priest, prophet, and judge in Israel. He anointed both Saul, the first king, and King David. We can imagine Hannah's joy in her old age knowing that was *her* son; the one "asked of God" was also given back to be *used* by God.

FURTHER REFLECTIONS

As we reflect on the whole span of Hannah's life, it doesn't hurt to revisit the place where we initially saw her. She was weeping before the Lord and praying out of the deep bitterness of her spirit. One of the notable disappointments in that scene is the insensitive reception she got from Eli. Let us hope that in our congregations of God's people, we can pour out our needs, the pain of our hearts, and our sorrow and shame in the presence of God who hears. And may we not deter those who seek this haven, emotionally broken as they—and we—are.

While Hannah was weeping and praying, she was also making a vow that would make most of us pause. It's remarkable, isn't it, that Hannah asked God to fulfill the deepest desire of her heart, and when he did, she gave it right back to him! I have to ask myself (again) how I can develop the trust that God will both give and receive back in the ways that are best. And to press the question a bit further, what are the things that I most long for? Are they things God would *want* to have given back to him? It is an ongoing challenge to *shape* the desires of our hearts so that they reflect God's heart. Hannah could, and did, because she knew her holy and utterly dependable God (1 Sam. 2:2).

TWELVE

Abigail: Married to a Foolish and Wicked Man

Biblical Text: 1 Samuel 25

Abigail was both beautiful and intelligent, but she was married to an absolute boor! We know this man's name as Nabal in our English Bibles. The Hebrew word is pronounced *naval* and it means "fool." This is not just any kind of fool. A *naval* is one who is hard-hearted and has no fear of God. Nabal was harsh, mean, and thought only of himself and his property. Chances are he considered Abigail part of that "property."

Abigail and Nabal lived in the southern part of the land of Judah. It is the kind of land where shepherds tended flocks of sheep and goats, roaming from place to place in order to find water sources and the best grazing. As a parallel, think of cowboys in the early American west, herding cattle on the range. Nabal was very wealthy and had 1,000 goats and 3,000 sheep.

BACKGROUND OF SAUL AND DAVID

To understand our story of Abigail, we need to enter the narrative a little bit before we actually meet her. Some years earlier, Saul had become the first king of Israel. In response to the word of the Lord, the prophet

Samuel first anointed Saul, and then he was also chosen by lot in a public gathering. This was clearly a significant development in the history of God's people. Prior to this, they had judges, priests, and prophets who served as their leaders. With the king, they would be like the nations around them. In fact, that is what they said when they clamored for a king. Being like everyone else, however, is not always the best choice!

For reasons we can only begin to guess, Saul disobeyed the word of the Lord—seriously and multiple times. It seems that a dreadful combination of pride and paranoia gathered their dark forces in his heart and he chose to go his own way rather than submitting to Samuel's instructions, which were from the Lord.

As a result, God commanded Samuel to anoint a very young David as the future king, even though Saul did continue to be king for a good number of years. In the meantime, David was successful and popular with nearly everyone. He was one of those people who could do just about everything. On the one hand, he was a skilled musician and performed on his harp in the court of Saul. He was a sensitive poet; about half the Psalms are attributed to David. At the same time, David killed Goliath and many other Philistines who were oppressing the Israelites. He was strong, courageous, and did not shy away from the brutality that is part of war.

The people loved David, which made Saul exceedingly jealous. Not only that; Saul's own son, Jonathan, who would have been in line to be the next king, loved David as if he were his own brother. In fact, Jonathan's love for David was truly self-sacrificial as his own father, Saul, did not hesitate to point out (1 Sam. 20:30-31).

Enraged and paranoid about losing his dynasty, Saul tried numerous times to kill David and finally David had to run for his life. He first went for refuge to the Philistines whose champion, Goliath, he had killed in battle. That did not last long! In fact, David was caught in between two enemies, both of whom were intent on getting rid of him. Finally, along with a number of loyal followers, he went to the south part of the country. They made their way along the edges of the settled areas, always on the run from Saul. Here is where the stories of David and Abigail come together.

DAVID'S REQUEST FOR "PAYMENT"

David came to the wilderness near where Nabal's shepherds were on the range. It was during the time of sheep shearing, which included much celebration. It was a community event; often-lonely shepherds—who had spent sleepless nights and dry, hot days watching the sheep—gathered to work together and swap stories. The atmosphere was full of the noises and smells of earthbound festivity. The sheep had been protected from all the dangers in the wilderness, and the prospect of a fresh lot of wool for tents and garments was within reach.

David sent ten of his young men bringing greetings to Nabal. He also told them to give Nabal a message. On this festive occasion, David said, it would be appropriate for Nabal to repay generously the care that David's men had provided for the sheep tenders. He expected Nabal to respond with characteristic gratitude and hospitality. As the story goes on, we find out that the servants of Nabal had been very thankful for the protection, saying it was like having a wall around them.

NABAL'S HARSH AND WICKED RESPONSE

Although Nabal heard the message, he spoke rudely about David and about his men. It was a complete put down in a culture where honor mattered. He acknowledged David's name and his father, Jesse, but said that this band was worse than scum. He refused to give them anything at all, saying "shall I take *my* bread and *my* water and *my* meat that I have killed for *my* shearers and give it to men who come from I do not know where?" (1 Sam. 25:11 ESV *italics mine*). Nabal had tightly clenched fists, not willing to let go of anything that he viewed as his.

This was not a coldhearted refusal to dole out charity, as unseemly as that would have been. Nabal's rejection of David's request was like refusing to pay a whole group of workers what they earned after weeks of employment. The men reported Nabal's words to David, who lost no time in preparing them to fight! This was looking really ugly because David took 400 armed men with him.

Word got back to Abigail by means of one of the servants who reported even more clearly what a help David and his men had been to them out in the wilderness. Nabal's harshness must have grated on his servants for a long time. On this occasion, the pent-up frustration came bursting out. They were not afraid to tell Abigail what a wicked man Nabal was and how impossible it was to reason with him. They knew better than anyone what disaster was coming upon them because they had come to know and respect David. It is also clear that they had great esteem for Abigail and trusted her to know what to do to stop this calamity from happening.

ABIGAIL'S WISE ACTIONS AND WORDS

Abigail *was* smart; she did know what to do and she did it immediately. She packed up the biggest festive dinner you could imagine. It included 200 loaves of bread, two large skins of wine, five sheep ready to cook and eat, five bushels of roasted grain, 100 cakes of raisins and 200 cakes of figs. All of this was loaded on donkeys—which gives us some picture of the extensive property of Nabal. It must have taken her some time to get this travelling feast ready, but the servants no doubt were working *very* quickly.

She sent the servants with all the goods ahead of her, perhaps to let David think Nabal had changed his mind. She also knew enough not to tell Nabal what she was doing. Off she went to meet David who was coming with all his men, intent on repaying her husband's shameful action. In fact, David said, "What a waste of time—all my watching over this fellow's property! It's been dangerous and we're exhausted. Because he has treated us wickedly, I swear none of his men will be alive by morning!" (1 Sam. 25:21-22, paraphrase). No wonder Nabal's servants feared for their very lives!

When Abigail got to David, she bowed down and pleaded with him to listen to her. She called herself David's servant, even though she was the wife of a large estate owner and David was a man fleeing for his life from the current government. Abigail also wisely shifted David's attention away from his intended vengeance by telling him that *she* would accept the blame. That worked, of course, because he would never attack a woman. She acknowledged what a wicked fool Nabal was.

While these may seem harsh and unwise words coming from the wife of a powerful man, they may in fact actually reveal the true misery of Abigail's life! She had utterly lost respect for him, and when it came to saving the lives of her whole household, she would speak honestly. She told David she had not been aware of his previous message to Nabal. She then very boldly *presumed* that David was no longer planning any destructive retaliation because, as she said, the Lord prevented him from doing it (1 Sam. 25:26). Once she made that declaration, there would be no way David could even think of his revenge. It would have been taking vengeance into his own hands instead of leaving it to the Lord. She added to that a somewhat odd blessing: May all your enemies be like Nabal. In other words, may God clear away all those who would oppose you. Then she produced the abundant "payment" of food and wine for David and his men.

Abigail's words and actions successfully stopped David from destroying Nabal and his people. She was quick to think of the right thing to do and she had the courage (as well as the means) to do it, approaching David even when he was burning with anger.

ABIGAIL ALSO SPOKE OF DAVID'S FUTURE

As Abigail concluded her plea to David, she said something with far-reaching implications, "The Lord will certainly make a lasting dynasty for you." Remember that by this time Samuel was dead; there was no prophetic voice for God's people. God used Abigail to speak prophetically, "The life of my master will be bound securely in the bundle of the living by the LORD your God" (1 Sam. 25:29). What a beautiful picture! Bundles contained important possessions so that they could be easily carried on journeys. This was life's journey and Abigail spoke of God's binding David into "bundle of the living" in spite of Saul's attempts to kill him.

Implicitly, she also warned him against becoming like Saul. He must not have wrongdoing in his background and on his conscience. She called it the "staggering burden of needless bloodshed" (1 Sam. 25:31). Abigail followed the picture of the securely bound bundle with a contrasting image regarding his enemies. They would be hurled away as a stone goes from the pocket of a sling, a visual picture that David would know well. He had proved himself with a slingshot in the battle with Goliath. Perhaps Abigail had heard of his actions and heroism in the face of the Philistine giant. Maybe she even knew that Samuel had anointed David to be the king. Samuel's journey to Bethlehem for that very purpose (1 Sam. 16:1–13) no doubt sent waves through the entire tribe of Judah where Abigail lived.

NABAL'S DEATH AND DAVID'S PROPOSAL

Immediately, David blessed Abigail for her good judgment in keeping him from taking vengeance. He accepted the payment and sent her on her way in peace. Abigail returned home to find Nabal holding a huge feast. He was very drunk. Having drunk too much is often linked in Bible stories with disaster to follow. This was true in Nabal's case as well. Abigail waited until morning to tell him what she had done. When she did, Nabal's heart failed him. About ten days later, he died (1 Sam. 25:38). When David heard of Nabal's death, he sent a message to Abigail asking her to be his wife.

In response, she again placed herself in a servant's position with her humble heart. She even offered to serve David's servants! She also did not waste any time, but left the whole estate of Nabal and went to David immediately. She took along five young women to attend to her needs.

This tiny detail gives us a glimpse into the dramatic change in store for Abigail. She had been accustomed to servants; now she was joining a rugged band of men who were considered outlaws in some circles. No doubt these women would be important not only as servants, but also as female companions.

FURTHER REFLECTIONS

We have to wonder about Abigail, her strong feelings against Nabal, and how trapped she must have felt the entire time she was married to him. As the wife of a wealthy man, she had everything that her nomadic culture and those surroundings could provide, and yet her life was miserable. Even so, we might think of all those experiences as preparation for this moment. She knew how to deal with rash anger. And thus, she knew how to handle the threat of David and was prepared to do so. God used her to preserve David's integrity so he would not have senseless bloodshed on his hands.

Did Abigail long to escape Nabal's cruelty? She obviously did not care to stay connected to his property or the clan once he had died. Perhaps there were sons who were more like Nabal and would treat her with contempt. Perhaps she feared reprisals for having given David a significant chunk of Nabal's property. Even though the servants clearly respected her, they would not have wielded much power to protect her had that been necessary. In any case, she left her past entirely and joined David, whom she recognized as having a royal future ahead of him.

Three things are worth observing from Abigail's life. First, she did not leave her marriage, even though it was, from everything we can see, grim. To be sure, that was not nearly as easy an option in that culture as it is today. Nevertheless, her faithfulness, difficult as it must have been, was also part of God's perfect design as he prepared her for this moment in David's life. This is a sobering but also encouraging thought. Second, she had the courage to confront David and speak the truth he needed to hear. We often find ourselves in situations where it would be much more comfortable *not* to challenge the impulsive plans of a powerful person. Abigail is a winsome example of humbly disarming destructive intentions. Third, once God rescued her from Nabal's household, Abigail left all of the accompanying wealth.

Let us examine our hearts to make certain that we hold loosely to the treasure this world offers. Of all things, we don't want to mirror Nabal's attitude toward our possessions, all of which are simply on loan to us from God.

THIRTEEN

Esther: For Such a Time as This

BIBLICAL TEXT: ESTHER

J ust as Abigail was prepared by God for a very significant moment, so also was Esther. We first meet Esther as an orphan; both her mother and father had died. She was a young Israelite woman in exile. One might say she had three strikes against her in that culture—female gender, no family, and a foreigner. When her story ends, however, she was a powerful queen of Persia. What happened in the interval is a wonderful story of God's providence, even though the name of God never appears in the book of Esther at all. Here is how the story unfolds.

XERXES AND THE JEWS IN THE PERSIAN EMPIRE

In order to understand the remarkable nature of Esther's position, we need to sketch a bit of Babylonian and Persian history. Xerxes (Ahasuerus in the Hebrew text) was the proud and powerful king of the mighty Persian Empire. The date of Xerxes' accession to the throne was 486 BC, about one hundred years after the Babylonians under King Nebuchadnezzar destroyed the temple in Jerusalem and took a significant number of Israelites into exile. The changes on the political landscape had been dramatic. About half a century after that power play of Nebuchadnezzar, the Babylonian empire was overrun by the Medes and Persians. In very short order, a rising star named Cyrus the Great issued a decree that people groups in his empire could return to their native lands and rebuild their temples.

One of the groups who benefited was the Jewish community in exile. We read their story in the first chapters of Ezra, where we learn that some had returned to their land and rebuilt the temple. On the other hand, many others stayed in Persia. The book of Esther is really their story as well as Esther's.

King Xerxes was planning to go to war against Greece—again. Xerxes' predecessor on the throne, Darius, had attempted to take Athens, only to lose at the battle of Marathon. When Darius died, Xerxes ascended the throne. Just about seven years had passed since Darius' venture and Xerxes needed to bolster support for the renewed war effort. In order to do this, he held a very long series of banquets for military brass from all over the kingdom to show off his wealth. Xerxes' arrogance and the extreme opulence of the Persian court are the targets of subtle humorous jabs in chapter 1 of Esther. We also know a good deal about Xerxes' unsavory character from the Greek historian Herodotus.

QUEEN VASHTI REFUSED TO OBEY THE KING

As part of Xerxes' display, he called for his wife Vashti to appear before all the men at the festival. She was beautiful, and he wanted to show off yet one more of his possessions. Since the text specifies that she was to be wearing her crown, ancient Jewish commentators suggested that Xerxes had asked her to appear with *only* her crown, a further lewd aspect of the all-male carousing. To Xerxes' dismay and shame, however, Vashti refused to exhibit herself. This made him so furious that he, the most powerful figure in the empire, was unable to decide what to do next!

Vashti had publicly dishonored the king, and her action could have severe repercussions for male honor, official and otherwise. The women of nobility would hear of the queen's shocking behavior and could brazenly use it to shame their own husbands. Thus, the king's advisers gave him their best counsel; Vashti was never to appear before him again! Appearing before him was, of course, what she refused to do in the first place. Even more ironic, this advice made permanent and *public* Vashti's own refusal to be in the king's presence at the banquet. It also effectively removed her from any sphere where she might in the future exercise power.

Xerxes depended on the wisdom of his young servants to determine how to find him a new queen. Their plan was to gather all the beautiful young virgins in the empire. Whichever one pleased the king the most would become queen. No doubt there would be a high level of sensual entertainment associated with the process.

The roundup of young virgins, one of antiquity's beauty pageants, would be conducted in the same officious manner as the rest of the Persian bureaucracy. A commission, responsible for getting all the likely prospects to the harem at Susa, was appointed to gather them from each province. The description of the operation makes it quite clear that local populations had no choice in the matter. We can imagine the deep uneasiness as family members watched their young women taken away.

ESTHER AND MORDECAI

At this point, we meet Esther and her cousin Mordecai. Esther was a young Israelite woman living in exile. Esther 2:7 emphasizes the absence of her parents, indicating twice that both had died. Except for her cousin Mordecai, who adopted her as his daughter, she would have been deserted. He cared for her and she was obedient to him. The description of Esther emphasizes her beauty—"beautiful of form" and "lovely in appearance" are a literal translation of the Hebrew (Esther 2:7). In other words, she was so beautiful it would have been impossible for her to avoid the roundup of young virgins for the king.

Neither she nor Mordecai would have been able to prevent it. When Esther was brought to the court of the king, she was worlds away from her Jewish home. Nevertheless, Mordecai made a daily practice of checking on her welfare.

ESTHER "WON FAVOR" WITH EVERYONE

Once Esther was in the court harem, she won favor with the servant who was in charge of the young women. His name was Hegai. He guided her through the whole year of preparation for her audience with Xerxes. There were oil massages for six months to soften her skin, a significant matter in a hot and dry climate. These were followed by treatment with spices for another six months. Each contestant could ask for anything she wished to take with her to the king's palace. When Esther's turn came, she took along only what Hegai advised. The narrative is beguilingly opaque at this point; we are not told what Hegai suggested, but the king was pleased with Esther, and she was crowned the next queen.

We are left to wonder how Esther felt about all of this; the story does not give us any clues. We do know that she was not a passive presence. The recurring expression, "won favor," (Esther 2:9, 15, 17) suggests that she was actively engaged in doing her best to be pleasing in every context.

HAMAN'S EVIL PLAN

At this point, Xerxes did not know Esther was Jewish. Mordecai had told her to keep that part of her identity under wraps, which implies he might have been aware of simmering prejudice.

Shortly after Esther's coronation, Mordecai discovered a plot to assassinate the king and reported it to Esther. Although the two culprits were publicly executed, Mordecai was never rewarded for exposing their conspiracy. Instead, a truly evil man named Haman was elevated by the king to be second in the power structure, possibly at the expense of recognizing Mordecai. At the same time, the multiple advisers that had previously been on the scene faded into the background. Haman was solidifying a powerful hold on the king.

As events unfolded, Xerxes seemed to be blind to the vile schemes of Haman, who was excessively egotistical and maneuvering to gain public recognition and honor at any cost. Haman was furious when he learned that Mordecai would not bow in his presence, even though the king commanded it. When Haman found out Mordecai was Jewish, he determined to ruin not only him, but all of the Jewish people. He told the king there was a dissident (nameless) group of people living throughout the empire. He claimed they were a threat to the stability of the realm because they refused to obey the king's laws, and should be destroyed. The king gave Haman permission to issue a decree that would allow the slaughter of these people in every part of the kingdom on a certain day. While Haman intended to target Jews, he did not name them in the king's presence and Xerxes remained appallingly oblivious. Because the decree was sent in multiple languages throughout the entire empire, there would be no safe haven.

ESTHER CHALLENGED TO SAVE HER PEOPLE

When the king's edict was made public, Mordecai went to the king's gate wailing and dressed in mourning clothes. His cry was so intense that it penetrated the regal façade of the court. No doubt quite embarrassed, Esther sent her servant to find out why her cousin was making such a scene. Through the servant, they carried on a conversation and Mordecai sent her a copy of the decree. He challenged Queen Esther to risk her life to save her people.

Esther explained that anyone who went into the king's presence without being invited could lose her life, unless the king extended his golden scepter. To emphasize the point, she said she had not been with the king for a month. Nothing good could come of this. Mordecai answered, in effect, if you remain silent, do you really think relief and deliverance will come from any other place? You and your father's family will die, even though you are the queen. In other words, you will be found out and all the rest of us will die as well. In fact, you are our only hope. Who knows but that you have come to the royal position *for such a time as this?* (Esther 4:13-14, author's paraphrase).

Many Scripture translations suggest that relief and deliverance *would* come from another place if Esther did not rise to the occasion. In fact, some suggest this is a subtle way of saying God would intervene. It is better, however, to translate the Hebrew as Mordecai's desperate question, not his declaration that there was a backup source of hope. This fits much better with the rest of his description of the consequences of the decree. As he saw it, Esther was the last hope for her people. Esther's dilemma was one repeated throughout history; she was hemmed in by circumstances and expected either death as the penalty for breaking the royal law or death at the hands of mob violence.

"FOR SUCH A TIME AS THIS"

"For such a time as this . . . " This was the critical moment for Esther and she chose publicly to identify with her people, even at the likely cost of her life. She showed her strength of character in her decision both to defy the king's law and to confront Haman, the second most powerful person in the empire. She took command, giving orders to Mordecai to mobilize their people.

Esther called for a corporate and comprehensive fast. This was grueling; there was to be neither eating *nor* drinking for three days and nights! It was a radical appeal for God's intervention. Esther further determined that her young women (who probably were not Jewish) would fast in the same manner along with her. Following that, she would enter into the king's presence.

Her closing words to Mordecai are telling. In spite of this dramatic corporate appeal for divine mercy, it seems she expected it to fail. It was, after all, contrary to the Persian law whose effects she knew first hand!

Her statement can equally well be translated, "when I perish, I perish," indicating her recognition that death was the likely outcome.

It was when things were hopelessly impossible that God used Esther in the position to which he had brought her. Her life had been painful. It is likely that the time in the court was not pleasant for a young Jewish woman. She was no doubt forced to do things against her convictions. She probably heard words that shocked her. And now she faced losing her life. Nevertheless, it was all part of a much larger plan. She did not know her action would result in the deliverance of the Jews but, out of conviction, she called for them to fast for three days and then she crossed the boundary into the king's chambers. And God, who does the impossible, moved the king to hold out the golden scepter to her.

ESTHER'S PLAN TO UNMASK HAMAN

Esther won the king's favor and then, in response to his question and promise of up to half his kingdom, piqued his curiosity by inviting him and Haman to a private banquet. Chances are the three days of fasting had also been three days of planning. This had to be done exactly right or it would not just fail; it would be catastrophic. After all, Haman was the second most powerful person in the empire and he could easily turn this treachery against her with a few slippery words. The king and Haman both came to the feast and again Esther tantalized them—and maybe roused the king's suspicion—by not answering him directly. Instead, she simply invited them to another private dining experience.

Haman headed home elated until he encountered Mordecai, who this time refused to rise in Haman's presence. First he would not bow; now he would not stand to attention. That sent Haman into another rage. Once he got home, his wife suggested that he arrange a public hanging for Mordecai. This restored Haman's good humor and he set up the pole on which to impale Mordecai. Then he went to the court to acquire the king's permission to get rid of Mordecai once and for all.

THE KING COULD NOT SLEEP

In the meantime, the king just happened to have a bout of insomnia; he could not sleep. Isn't it interesting how one simple circumstance dramatically changed the direction of the entire narrative? Even though the name of God does not appear in the whole book of Esther, here are his "fingerprints." Although Esther and Mordecai were carefully planning the best way to rescue their people, it was something entirely out of their hands that turned the tables. Only God could have brought about the sleepless restlessness of the king (Esther 6:1).

In order to help Xerxes fall back to sleep, the court chronicles were read to him. There could not have been a better cure for insomnia! But before he nodded off, the chronicles just happened to cover the incident five years before, when Mordecai exposed the plot to kill the king. Xerxes was very distressed to discover he had neglected to reward Mordecai. He determined to set matters right because it was, in effect, a dishonor to the king himself to have neglected such a thing. At that very moment, Haman happened to arrive at Xerxes' bedroom door to ask permission to hang Mordecai.

HONOR AND SHAME

Before Haman could make his request, the king asked Haman what should be done for the person the king wished to honor. In his self-centered arrogance, Haman was certain the king intended this recognition for him. He described an elaborate ceremony complete with royal robe and horse, and a crier who went ahead announcing that this person was favored by the king. Imagine how humiliated Haman was when he then had to perform this ceremony for Mordecai (Esther 6:11)!

No doubt the people who watched the procession in the public square were acutely aware of the tension between the two men. Mordecai's refusal to bow had not occurred in private. Many people may also have become increasingly dismayed at the effects of Haman's excessive pride. Seeing him shamed probably felt like justice done. Haman got home just in time to be escorted back to the second banquet Esther had prepared for him and the king. We don't know if she had heard of the doings in the public square. She may have instead been working on her script for the evening's drama, painfully aware of the weighty responsibility that rested on her every word.

ESTHER REVEALED HAMAN'S EVIL PLAN

After they had dined together, the king was ready to hear Esther. Banquets were long and there had been a significant amount of time for tension to build. The king may have wondered why Esther was paying equal attention to Haman by inviting him to each banquet. Was there something afoot? This was the third time the king asked to know Esther's request and he again promised to grant her petition entirely. His words were significant, "What is your wish? It shall be granted. What is your request? Even up to half my kingdom, it shall be fulfilled" (Esther 7:2, ESV).

Following the lead of the king and perhaps in keeping with court etiquette, Esther expressed her response in corresponding pairs. Knowing that her own life was more significant as far as the king was concerned, she first asked that her life be granted as her wish and then her people as her request. His honor would, after all, be profoundly damaged if the queen were killed in conjunction with Haman's edict against the Jews.

The next part of her plea was a masterpiece in diplomacy. She had to set the stage for the accusation of Haman without implicating the king who was, to be sure, equally culpable in the matter. Haman was the king's choice as second in the realm, and the king had granted him free reign to unleash his fury against the Jews. In declaring, "We have been sold, I and my people," Esther identified herself with the Jews even though she did not yet name them. Her direct quote of the decree—"for destruction and slaughter and annihilation" (Esther 7:4) —did away with any ambiguity; at this point Haman would have realized, with mounting horror, what this meant for him.

Esther's use of the term "sold" had multiple layers of meaning. The Jews had been "delivered over" (literally "sold") for destruction; they had also actually been sold as Haman had offered the king money for their annihilation and Xerxes appears to have accepted. Even sale into slavery, Esther maintained, would have been tolerable and she would have kept quiet. Why? Because if she were sold into slavery by an edict sanctioned by the king himself, it would have been unthinkably shameful. When Esther pointed this out, she put the matter in stark terms of the king's own honor. Now that it was public, he had to respond.

Notably, the king did not recognize the language of the decree or make the connection between Esther's reference and Haman. Because he had been negligent in knowing about Haman's real activities and the identity of his queen, he asked the question that allowed Esther to point at Haman. "Who is he? Where is the man who has dared to do such a thing?" (Esther 7:5).

Esther's response, "this vile Haman" (Esther 7:6), infuriated the king. He had been duped by Haman in more ways than one, and Esther's own subterfuge might have irritated him to a degree. How humiliating that his own queen identified herself with a people officially consigned to destruction! His enraged exit matched his character. Haman turned to Esther to plead for his life. He knew the king had decided his fate (Esther 7:7), but perhaps he hoped the king again would not act on his own. If so, Esther was his only and very slim hope.

In the final irony, Haman fell onto the couch where Esther, the Jewish queen, was reclining. He was in that posture of entreaty when the king returned and found him there. Whether the king deliberately misinterpreted this action, or actually thought Haman was assaulting Esther, is unclear. What the king saw allowed him to make a charge that would resolve his dilemma about the personally embarrassing implications of his edict. Everything could be blamed on Haman. In a tidy demonstration of measure-for-measure justice, Haman would die because of a false accusation just as he had falsely accused the Jews.

THE END OF *THIS* STORY

Together Esther and Mordecai countered the deadly decree of Haman with a royal authorization for the Jews to defend themselves in the face of organized, empire-wide attacks on their persons and property. They were successful, and a commemorative celebration called Purim was established. The biblical account ends with peace and stability reigning throughout the land.

FURTHER REFLECTIONS

As the narrative unfolds, Esther's character develops from what appears to be an initially submissive charge of her cousin to a remarkable authority figure. It is clear that from the moment she set foot in the harem, she was an *actor* within the wider machinery of the royal household and the court. The hint to this effect lies in the Hebrew idiom translated "she won favor," which appears repeatedly in chapter 2. This is a more dynamic expression than the usual "found favor." This says something about how she conducted herself both in public and in private. Although we are not told the specifics of her words and actions in the harem, we can guess from her later activities that she was diplomatic, tactful, and also very wise in terms of when to talk and when to keep silent. No doubt she learned to set aside frustrations, annoyances, and even her own deep sense of personal loss and displacement. They might have bred bitterness, but Esther did not nurse them. Instead, she nurtured good relationships. As a result, the people around her were eager to help when she needed them. Perhaps part of winning favor is also knowing when to have the humility to ask for help.

Esther's story leaves us with deep admiration for her courage in the midst of extremely dangerous circumstances. The central theological truth in Esther is that all the plans of humans cannot overturn the sovereign will of God that his chosen people survive. Nevertheless, these providential "coincidences," numerous as they are, are lodged in contexts that demand responsible and faithful human choices and action. Sometimes God's people are forced to make decisions even though every option seems fraught with uncertainty and God's purposes seem hidden.

Our task is first to spend the necessary time seeking God's wisdom and intervention, as Esther did when she took upon herself the discipline of three days of fasting. We might add earnest prayer as well! And then we step forward in trust and obedience, convinced that God will accomplish his perfect will. After all, Esther challenges all readers to consider in what manner God has prepared each of us "for such a time as this."

FOURTEEN

Called by God to Speak His Word

BIBLICAL TEXTS: 2 KINGS 22–23; 2 CHRONICLES 34–25;
PSALM 68; JOEL 2:12–32; ACTS 2

Did you ever think of yourself as a prophet? Most likely not, unless you just happened to "predict" some unexpected outcome and your friends lightheartedly congratulated you when that event did indeed occur. And yet, there is a sense in which we are all called to be prophets. But what does that mean, and how on earth might you and I fit into that role?

THE GIFT OF PROPHECY: SPEAKING GOD'S WORD

We customarily think of prophets as telling the future, either dramatically announcing events that will change the course of world history or perceptively telling some unsuspecting individual what she will do tomorrow afternoon. In the Old Testament, however, prophets were people who knew the Word of the Lord and were called by God to speak that Word primarily to fellow Israelites. It was that simple—and difficult! Their most important task was to warn hardened skeptics that judgment was indeed coming; there were limits to God's forgiving love.

Today this might mean speaking boldly in church contexts where complacency and self-serving attitudes have sapped the vitality from the gospel message. Or it might mean a wise and winsome voice in the wider culture, directing troubled and broken souls to the Source of justice and hope.

Messages of judgment are rarely popular. Often those who have the prophetic task thrust upon them are ridiculed and caricatured. It takes a full measure of the discerning Spirit and good dose of humility to address our own flaws effectively and then gently prod others where it might hurt. At the same time, the prophetic voice also encourages faithful people to *stay* faithful in spite of suffering and doubt. This is a pattern we are still called to follow.

Because prophets, both women and men, were generally called to speak to God's people under dire circumstances, we always need to understand the course of events that brought these courageous individuals to their high-profile positions. We also need to be reminded that the prophets did not speak out of their own imaginations. They were "carried along by the Holy Spirit" (2 Pet. 1:21), and their words had power.

THE PROPHET HULDAH

In the years shortly before God's people were torn from their homeland and marched off into exile in a foreign land, they were in desperate need of the kind of warning we have been talking about. They worshiped idols; they had forsaken God and broken the covenant. Lest we think that these problems are lodged solely in the dustbins of antiquity, it is worth reminding ourselves of what the apostle Paul said: Greed is idolatry (Col. 3:5). Oops; time to recalibrate.

At any event, the king at the time was Josiah, a godly man who did what was right in the eyes of the Lord (2 Kings 22). While in his twenties, he gave orders to clean up and repair the temple of the Lord. Hilkiah, the high priest, found the book of the Law as they were shoveling out the piles of worthless idols that had accumulated, of all places, in the temple. It says something about the people that they had "lost" God's covenant Word amidst the clutter of contemporary trappings that were apparently more relevant and appealing in their increasingly pluralistic culture. We, of course, would never lose the Bible as we swim in our cultural pools—or have we already done so? Do we rob the word of God of its resurrection power by keeping it safely under wraps, confined to those ten minutes each morning?

When the book was read in the king's presence, Josiah was horrified and tore his robes, a sign of remorse and repentance. He knew the whole cultural fabric was stained with criminal offenses, many of them perpetrated by his own father, Manasseh. Leaders and common folk alike were guilty of the kinds of things that another contemporary prophet, Habakkuk, complained about to God: "Destruction and violence are before me; strife and contention arise. So the law is paralyzed and justice never goes forth" (Hab. 1:3-4, ESV). Sound familiar?

Josiah immediately called for someone to interpret the words of the text they had found. Notably, Hilkiah the priest and major court officials did not confer among themselves and send back an opinion. They did not summon Jeremiah from the small suburb just north of the city. Instead, they went to a woman named Huldah who lived right in Jerusalem. It is quite clear that she was an authoritative teacher and was also known as a prophet, one through whom the Lord spoke.

Huldah told them to take a message from the Lord back to the king, "This is what the LORD says: 'I am going to bring disaster on this place and its people, according to everything written in the book the king of Judah has read. Because they have forsaken me and burned incense to other gods and provoked me to anger by all the idols their hands have made, my anger will burn against this place and will not be quenched'" (2 Kings 22:16-17).

That was not news; it was already in the book. Then she sent a message for the king himself, "Because your heart was responsive and you humbled yourself before the LORD when you heard what I have spoken against this place and its people, that they would become accursed and laid waste, and because you tore your robes and wept in my presence, I have heard you, declares the LORD. I will gather you to your fathers and you will be buried in peace. Your eyes will not see all the disaster I am going to bring on this place" (1 Kings 22:19-20). This declaration was reassuring to Josiah, to be sure, but slim comfort regarding his people. And in fact, Josiah himself would die in battle against the forces of Egypt; the promised "peace" was a relative matter.

THE RESPONSE TO HULDAH'S MESSAGE

In response, Josiah called together all the people of Judah and Jerusalem (2 Kings 23). It was a big town hall event. He read the covenant to them and then they all promised to follow the Lord and keep his commandments. Promise was followed by zealous action. They cleaned up the temple and took out all the false idols that were in it. They got rid of evil priests and foreign altars. Josiah commanded the people to celebrate Passover, their great festival to remember how God had redeemed them from slavery in Egypt. That deliverance symbolized their freedom from enslavement to sin. Now they were celebrating release from their bondage to idol worship and false gods.

No wonder that every time there was a revival in ancient Israel, they went back to the basics and celebrated Passover. No wonder that Jesus accomplished his work on the cross at the time of Passover and paid that price of his own Lamb's blood to buy us back from slavery to the forces of evil.

There had not been such a great Passover celebration in all of Israel's history as the one that Josiah held (2 Kings 23:22). God again had mercy on the Israelites and spared them during Josiah's reign. Tragically, the results of that profoundly moving and effective ceremony were painfully short-lived. Josiah died. His sons followed him in quick succession, each one of them doing evil in the eyes of the Lord. And in less than a decade, they were headed for destruction.

Here's a point for us: It was the word of Huldah, as she fearlessly told the king how severely the people of Judah would suffer, that ignited the national movement toward righteousness. We have to wonder what happened to Huldah in the years that followed. Did she join a protest movement as the fervor of the revival quickly faded? What was she able to do as everything around her fell apart? We know Jeremiah's desolation; his anguish is palpable both in the book that bears his name and in the book of Lamentations. Perhaps Huldah joined him in his attempts to stop the nation in its reckless downward spiral.

We know little else of Huldah other than her husband's pedigree. She was sufficiently well-known that five of the top religious leaders of the day consulted with her. Her place of residence in "the second quarter" (2 Kings 22:14) likely indicates a later addition to the main city of Jerusalem, perhaps west of the Temple complex. The term, also used in Zephaniah 1:10, may suggest more upscale living. Otherwise, why mention her address? Whatever the case, she did not mince words, but confronted these leaders with the disobedience and idolatry of the people. The five leaders would not have been entirely innocent in this matter; it was the priests' responsibility to teach the people God's word and they had obviously failed to do so effectively. Huldah did not hesitate to declare God's judgment on the people as well as his grace toward Josiah. Not an easy message; this vignette speaks volumes about a faithful woman.

We All Proclaim God's Word

If we think that only extraordinary women like Huldah are ever called to speak the word of God, Psalm 68:11 comes as a delightful surprise, "The Lord announced the word, and great was the company of those who proclaimed it." While the significance of this verse may not be apparent at first glance, the original language reveals truth that extends to each one of us.

The expression in English, "those who proclaimed it," does not tell all that is embedded in the Hebrew, which happens to be one single word rather than four. It is a feminine form of the word, meaning that God gives the same privilege of proclaiming his word to women as he does to men. In fact, women are front and center here. How do we know that? It works like this. Hebrew verbs have either masculine or feminine forms. When they are used in conjunction with mixed gender groups, they are generally masculine to cover all the bases. But this verb form, translated "those who proclaimed (or "are proclaiming") it," is feminine. In other words, *women* have the joy of hearing, knowing, and announcing God's words of grace and forgiveness. We are truly part of a "great company" of preachers. Several verses later in that same Psalm we read, "Praise be to the Lord, to God our Savior, who daily bears our burdens" (verse 19). Now that's a message we can deliver with confidence! Who would not want to hear of a loving Father who carries what we are unable to bear?

YOUR SONS AND DAUGHTERS WILL PROPHESY

Just about six hundred years before Christ, the prophet Joel anticipated the participation of women in the ministry of preaching the Good News. Joel 2:28–32 promises that in the last days, God will pour out his Spirit on all people. "Your sons and daughters will prophesy, your old men will dream dreams, and your young men will see visions. Even on my servants, both men and women, I will pour out my Spirit in those days. I will show wonders in the heavens and on the earth, blood and fire and billows of smoke. The sun will be turned to darkness and the moon to blood before the coming of the great and dreadful day of the LORD. And everyone who calls on the name of the LORD will be saved."

Those "last days" of which Joel spoke actually seem to span the entire church age, starting with the remarkable outpouring of God's Spirit at Pentecost and ending with the grand apocalypse at the end of this age. The important point, however, is that *everyone* who calls on the name of the Lord will be saved. And a second point is that there are no gender or age distinctions among messengers; we may all have the joy of declaring the good news of the gospel.

THE OUTPOURING OF THE HOLY SPIRIT

Immediately after the resurrection and ascension of Jesus, the believers, including women, gathered for earnest prayer (Acts 1:14) and their numbers increased. Jesus' followers were soon joined by thousands of Jews gathered for the festival of Pentecost (Acts 2). Pentecost, also called the feast of Harvest (Exod. 23:14–17) and Weeks (Deut. 16:9–12), was one of the three Jewish festivals during which God's people were commanded to go to Jerusalem. That meant whole families would be there, just as they were when Jesus went with his family up to Jerusalem for Passover. What a perfect set-up! Here were throngs of obedient and faithful Jewish pilgrims coming to rejoice in God's presence, remember their deliverance from Egypt, and recall God's giving the Torah from Mt. Sinai. The book of Acts tells us that Jews from all over the Roman Empire and beyond had congregated in the city. They had no idea that this Pentecost season would change their lives forever.

All of a sudden a sound like a violent wind filled the whole place. While the word "house" is used, it likely refers to the temple. That would be where all the pilgrims congregated for the festival celebration. But the rushing wind was not all. Flames of fire came to rest on the believers who were also gathered there. They were filled with the Holy Spirit and began to speak in other languages (Acts 2:2–4). This was God's precious gift; the visitors to Jerusalem all heard the message in their own languages. Some who heard the noise poked fun at the believers for having enjoyed their wine a bit too much, but the apostle Peter stood up and said, "This is what Joel was talking about!" Then he quoted the Joel 2 passage from start to finish—"and *everyone* who calls on the name of the Lord will be saved." And this was only the beginning. The ministry continued and expanded, empowered by the Holy Spirit. These dynamic congregations included women as they spoke the powerful Word (Acts 4:31).

FURTHER REFLECTIONS

God does work through the faithful responses of his people. Huldah spoke the truth to some of the most high-profile men in the government and she did so without flinching. It would have been a lot easier to sugarcoat the sober message of God's judgment, especially when that message was going to the king! But Huldah knew these were not her own words; they were straight from Scripture and she was compelled to apply that truth to the dire circumstances of her day. May God grant us both the discipline to learn what Scripture says and the winsome presence to articulate transforming truth to a needy world!

Following the drama of Pentecost, the growing band of believers in Jesus—including women—devoted themselves to the teaching of the apostles, to fellowship, to communal meals, and to prayer. As the assembly expanded, they continued to meet in the temple courts and ate together in homes (Acts 2:41–47); they spoke the Word (Acts 4:31), *and* they reached out to the suffering people around them (Acts 5:12–16). What a wonderful picture of the people of God, both then and today!

Continuing the Journey

It has been our privilege to trace the footprints left by dear saints from centuries past. In many ways, our journeys parallel theirs. Anxiety, disappointment, bitterness, and tragedy still dog our paths. At the same time, God's faithfulness has not diminished one bit and we can trust him to be our perfect guide and guardian.

In closing, let us revisit and cherish some highlights from our travels with these women. With Mary, we can memorize the Scriptures and *sing* them with joy when our expectations and hopes seem to crumble around us. And it did not stop there. Mary followed Jesus—all the way to the foot of the cross. So must we.

Sarah and Hagar challenge us to transcend the ever-present impulses that arise when jealousy rears its ugly head. Hagar's lowest point as she fled from Sarah gives us the clue as to how. God was present with her especially in that threatening wilderness. He is present with us even when we are wandering and feeling utterly lost. I repeat—God is with us.

When we are tempted as Rebekah was, to micro-manage the lives of those close to us, let us remind ourselves that our all-powerful God will bring about his perfect purposes and those are best done in his way. This often takes a very intentional pause in order to refocus. We need God's help daily; he does not *need* ours, but invites us to work *with* him.

The life of Deborah reminds us of the responsibilities of leadership. Deborah knew and understood her land and her people. They knew that she listened to and spoke for God and therefore, they trusted her judgment. Our challenge is to be wise in practical ways so that when opposition comes that threatens the safety and well-being of God's people, we are prepared and courageous.

A more heart-wrenching image lies in the footprint of Samson's mother as she watched her son reject everything that was part of his God-ordained Nazirite vow. The narrative does not tell us how she responded; we can only guess. But perhaps the same faith she expressed at the outset of the story bore her through those long years when Samson was at the end of his tether. As she heard of his violence and vengeance, and of his dalliances with Philistine women, she could only trust that God was using even those things for his purposes. That was true (Judg. 14:4), and it still is.

Naomi's sorrow and bitterness turned to hope when she experienced the faithful and loyal love of Ruth, her sole traveling companion on the way home. May we be that same kind of steady and encouraging presence for those whose hopes have been dashed by one tragedy after another!

Hannah unhesitatingly gave back to God what she had most dearly longed for and earnestly prayed for. Her life inspires us to take a sober look, daily and moment by moment, at the things we want most. Would they be appropriate and precious gifts back to God?

As we track Abigail through the wilderness of her life with a heartless man, we are reminded that those years prepared her to face David's anger with composure and wisdom. It seems to be the same lesson seen through yet another prism. God uses *everything* to accomplish his sovereign purposes. We see, again and again, that the impossible is indeed possible with God.

The same can confidently be said in regard to Esther. From the margins of society, God brought her to an astonishingly influential position in order to be ready "for such a time as this." Let us seek prayerfully to discern why we are where we are, and then commit ourselves to action on behalf of those whose lives and well-being are threatened, whether by external persecution or internal torment.

Our final lessons come from those women, named and nameless, who faithfully proclaimed God's word. Isn't it odd that we are so often reticent about declaring the most wonderful news that we could possibly bring to our troubled world? Let us set aside our fears in this regard, rest in the empowering presence of the Holy Spirit, and join those hosts of women who have been and are heralds of God's coming kingdom.

Questions for Discussion and Reflection

BY MEREDITH NYBERG, PHD

The question sets below are designed for both group discussion and individual reflection. These questions invite us to review together and remind each other of key parts of the stories. They also encourage us to explore additional connections within the fabric of biblical truth and consider how we respond to them. Some questions tap into personal experiences and emotions that may need to remain stored in our own hearts. All press us toward application of God's truth to our lives.

CHAPTER ONE: MARY, MOTHER OF GOD

1. What is the significance of Luke's repetition that Mary was a virgin (Luke 1:27, 34)? How does Mary's experience compare to the pregnancy of her older relative Elizabeth?

2. Have you ever felt rejected by "proper society," as Mary and Joseph no doubt felt? If you were driven to rely on God during that time, what nudged you in that direction?

3. Imagine how you would respond if an angel appeared proclaiming God's favor (Luke 1:28, 30). What was so disturbing about the angel's words to Mary (Luke 1:26–38)? What was reassuring?

4. Does Isaiah 9:6–7 help you to understand the angel's declaration? How can a *baby* be called "Wonderful Counselor, Mighty God, Everlasting Father, Prince of Peace" (Luke 1:32–33)?

5. In what ways did Mary share the reversals and humiliations that were the fabric of Jesus's life? Do you agree that "nothing is impossible with God" (Luke 1:37)? *Does that affirmation ground your intent to accept God's will for the rest of your life?* If not, what might be standing in the way?

CHAPTER TWO: MARY'S TRUST IN GOD'S TRUTH

1. Give yourself a window of time to contemplate what the meeting of Mary and Elizabeth was like (Luke 1:39–45). How would Elizabeth's prophetic words have encouraged Mary?

2. How does Mary's song proclaim God's power to turn our selfish expectations upside down (reread Luke 1:46–55, along with Hannah's song in 1 Sam. 2:1–10)?

3. How can we help each other learn to process our circumstances through the unfailing truth of Scripture as Mary and Elizabeth did? What passages from the Old Testament have you found helpful? In what ways?

4. For both Elizabeth and Mary, becoming a mother carried joy but also sadness. One was so young and vulnerable; the other would not live long enough to see her son grow to adulthood. In your own experience, when has life contained both promise and pain? What has steadied you during those times?

5. Mary had her baby in Bethlehem (Luke 2:4–7; Matt. 2:1–11), but perhaps the time and place described here are not what you had previously imagined. How were God's purposes served by this birthplace and by the first visitors, the shepherds of Bethlehem (Luke 2:8–18)?

6. Expecting our Christian lives to be free of pain is a recipe for disappointment. Instead, consider the times you experienced God's loving purposes through circumstances that were brimming with

uncertainty and anguish. Can you put your story into words that will encourage others?

CHAPTER THREE: MOTHERING GOD IN HIS EARLY YEARS

1. Simeon's prophetic message about Jesus had implications far beyond Mary's time and place, and yet he spoke personally to Mary (Luke 2:30–35). How do you think she managed to reconcile the joy and agony of those words?

2. King Herod seems to have acted out of "deep paranoia." Have you ever experienced the effects of fear warping a powerful person's mind? How were you able to address it? How was the response of the wise men (Magi) to the prophetic words of Micah radically different from that of Herod?

3. God chose to guide both the wise men and Joseph through dreams. In addition to God's Word, in what ways does God guide people today? Do some ways seem more reliable than others? How are we to know?

4. What must it have been like to be the mother of a perfect child who never sinned? Remember this child was also the Son of God (Luke 1:35). Can you imagine the tangle of love, humility, and awe as Mary parented her Son? What lessons might we apply to our own parenting experiences?

5. Consider prayerfully what treasured memories you hold in your heart that remind you of God's personal love for you. Do you draw on them to give you deep assurance through the trying times that we all encounter?

CHAPTER FOUR: DASHED EXPECTATIONS

1. Why do you think Mary prompted Jesus to demonstrate his power

at the wedding in Cana? How did she show that she believed in him (John 2:1–12)?

2. When Jesus read Isaiah 61:1–2 in Nazareth, what was the significance of his explaining this Scripture as fulfilled "today" and his comments afterward (Luke 4:14–30)? Think about Mary's awkward position when the situation turned ugly. How would you have responded?

3. How would you feel if you were Mary and wanted to speak to your busy son? Would you understand his response (Matt. 12:46–50)? Remember Simeon's gentle warning—there would be a sword through Mary's soul, no doubt more than once.

4. What emotions must have torn Mary's heart, especially as she followed her Son on the "road to the cross"? Where do you turn for comfort in the midst of devastating circumstances? Have the Psalms been particularly meaningful to you?

5. Jesus considered Mary's welfare even as he was dying on the cross, asking John to care for his mother (John 19:26–27). What else did Mary see and hear as she stood near the foot of the cross? "Had the promises failed"?

6. Have you ever wondered just when Mary heard the good news of Jesus's resurrection and how she responded? Her life journey to that point had been an unimaginable roller coaster with the agonizing death of her Son as the absolute bottom. Yet, it seems she clung stubbornly to her hope in God's faithfulness. Take some time to summarize what you have learned from Mary's life as we know it through the Scriptures. What stands out the most to you?

CHAPTER FIVE: SARAH AND HAGAR

1. How do you imagine Sarai responded when Abram was suddenly called by God to move to Canaan (Gen. 12:1–5)? In your current

journey, has God led you to a new place or situation? What is your customary response to change, and are there new patterns you might nurture to build your trust in the God who does the impossible?

2. When moving to Egypt, Abram asked Sarai to claim to be his sister—do you agree that he was being protective of family honor, and that Sarai was blessed for her obedience to his plan (Gen. 12:10–20)? How does this compare to other possible interpretations?

3. Back in Canaan, Sarai had what seemed like a good idea—to acquire a child through the socially acceptable practice of joining her husband to her handmaid (Gen. 16:1–5). Did her plan work out well? How do we also try to direct the purposes of God? Can you recall instances when well-meaning nudging had unfortunate consequences?

4. How do you think Sarah heard the declaration "is anything too difficult for the LORD" (Gen. 18:14)? How do those words echo into your own circumstances?

5. How did Hagar face the later challenge of being sent away by Abraham with her son Ishmael? How did God meet her despair this time (Gen. 21:8–21)? Is it difficult for you to trust God when it seems like everyone is against you and you're in a "hopeless place"?

6. Consider the intertwined lives of Sarah and Hagar. How can we avoid becoming bitter when we are compelled to live with irritating people and circumstances that vex us on a daily basis? What strategies can we employ to learn grace, patience, and forgiveness?

CHAPTER SIX: REBEKAH, LEAH, AND RACHEL

1. Rebekah had a choice to make—continue life as usual or agree to marry Isaac and leave everything that was familiar (Gen. 24:1–61). It takes courage to follow God's will. In the past, have you tended to choose comfort or courage? What were the results?

2. The LORD answered Isaac's prayer for Rebekah to have children, and during her tumultuous pregnancy the LORD answered Rebekah when she went to consult him (Gen. 25:19–23). In what ways is it encouraging to you to know that God was intimately involved in the lives of Isaac, Rebekah, and their twin sons (Rom. 9:10–14)? Can you describe circumstances in which the LORD has clearly responded to your prayers?

3. Do you consider yourself impulsive like Esau or calculating and careful like Jacob (Gen. 25:24–34)? How would you describe the results of each of those character traits for the twins? Is there anything redeeming about these characteristics? How do we avoid the consequences of resentment (Heb. 12:14–17)?

4. Favoritism is a deadly matter that disrupts families, classrooms, and close friends, yet we fall into it so easily. Have you been in a situation where you played favorites and it wounded someone else, or where someone hurt you by favoring another?

5. What destructive family patterns do you see across the generations from Abraham and Sarah to Isaac and Rebekah, then to Esau and Jacob and their wives? Have you been part of overcoming a destructive family pattern? What part did prayer play in that? How did you persevere when change seemed long in coming?

CHAPTER SEVEN: GOD'S PLAN INCLUDED FOREIGN WOMEN

1. Even in the most loving of families, people hurt each other. How did Joseph's family members—who were not exactly loving to start with—wound one another, and what were the results (Gen. 37:1–36)? Consider your own family wounds and think about what might bring healing.

2. Sold as a slave in Egypt, Joseph might have thought he was at the lowest place, but then he was jailed for a crime he did not commit

(Gen. 39:1–23). When you were in a dark place in your life, did it seem as if things got even worse? How long did it take for the LORD to turn things around? Or are you still waiting? How were you able to hang on to the hope that God was working for you behind the scenes?

3. When Joseph's brothers finally confessed their unjust actions against him after their father died, what was his response (Gen. 50:15–21)? Do the words of Genesis 50:20 reveal a long-simmering resentment or a heart of forgiveness? If it is indeed true that "love and forgiveness that build on the affirmation of God's sovereignty are the only antidotes to the ugly thorns of bitterness and resentment," how can we put this into practice in our own situations?

4. When the two midwives Shiphrah and Puah feared God and lied to Pharaoh to save the babies of Israel, God rewarded them with families of their own (Exod. 1:15–21), and when Jochebed hid her baby, going against Pharaoh's edict, Moses was saved in Pharaoh's own household (Exod. 2:1–8). What does this show that God values above all? How do we apply this deep concern for life in each of our day-by-day dealings?

5. As a grown man, Moses carried three identities—Israelite, Egyptian, and Midianite. At earlier stages of his life, Egyptian and Midianite were more prominent, but then God personally met him (Exod. 3:1–15). In a culture focused on identity politics, how does our identity as children of God distinguish us? What challenges might it pose?

6. How was the choice that Rahab of Jericho made (Josh. 2:1–24; 6:16, 22–25) similar to that of Moses? How was it different, especially as she intentionally made both cultural and social shifts? Can you relate?

7. When reflecting on "the unwelcome treatment outsiders often receive from the likes of us," consider—are there people outside of your comfortable circle whom you can encourage and from

whom you can learn? Look around with sensitivity and compassion. Without naming names, how can you intentionally "love your neighbor" (Lev. 19:18; Matt. 22:39)?

CHAPTER EIGHT

1. Both Deborah and Barak were leaders. It seems that Deborah had a higher "national" profile. Barak did not appear to resent that but, in fact, asked for her presence and help. How refreshing that is! How can we encourage those around us who bring a wide range of gifts, abilities, sensitivities, and fears to be courageous in the LORD's calling?

2. In that ancient Israelite culture, Barak's lack of courage meant a loss of honor for him, notably in the victory over the enemy general being given to a woman (Jael). How should we "translate" that into our twenty-first-century contexts?

3. Did you notice in this chapter a return to trust in the face of apparently overwhelming odds? Reflect on circumstances in your own life where you were driven back into the strong, everlasting arms because, quite frankly, there was no where else to turn. What did God's Spirit use to encourage you to trust sooner and more fully in that challenging time?

4. To sing is to teach. What echoes of our culture (silly commercials?) stick in your head whether you want them to or not? Why are they so stubbornly there? How have you gone about trying to get rid of them?

5. As an alternative, think of one chorus, hymn, or other musical expression of biblical truth that has given you hope, comfort, and joy (or all the above). Try singing it out loud until it continues to be in your heart. Why do you think the combination of music, rhythm, and well-chosen words works so well?

CHAPTER NINE

1. Reread Judges 13 and think about the responses of Samson's mother and her husband, Manoah, to the appearance(s) and message of the angel of the LORD. Why might they have reacted differently? What lesson is clear in her declaration in verse 23?

2. Two times the angel instructed Samson's mother to abstain from the restricted practices as she prepared to give birth to her son, a future Nazirite (see Numbers 6). What do you think this previously barren woman felt as she held herself to those limitations? Joy? Determination? What about later, when all her dedication was turned upside down by Samson's persistent rebellion?

3. Samson's choices were lethal; how can we avoid the same kinds of pitfalls? At the same time, Judges 14:4 makes it clear that Samson's choices were *not* outside the sovereign will of the LORD. What reassurance (and challenge) does that pose for us, especially if we are parents?

4. What are the most tempting aspects of our wider culture for you? Another way of putting this would be "How do you spend your time and your money, and what do you hope to achieve with that 'investment'?" Why are you (we) drawn to these "Timnahs" and beyond? How can we redirect our compulsions and desires?

5. Samson's mother may have wondered how to intervene as she saw her son deliberately rebelling. When you see someone you love dearly heading down the path to "the Philistines," what will you do?

CHAPTER TEN

1. Unfailingly loyal covenant love (*hesed*) shaped each of the three main characters—Ruth, Naomi, and Boaz—so that their daily choices were made in consideration of the needs of others. What

did Boaz sacrifice and why? How about Ruth? Can you find parallels between their choices and what you encounter each day?

2. What are three areas of your life in which you are regularly challenged to put your own desires second for the good of your family, your friends, your coworkers? What has helped you do this?

3. How does Naomi's honesty serve as a model for you? Are there limits to expressions of bitterness?

4. Do you think the women of Bethlehem might have feared Naomi had given up on God? How would you come alongside someone in Naomi's position?

5. What might be a modern-day counterpart to Ruth's daily gleaning work in the field to provide for her mother-in-law? Ask the same question regarding her venture to the threshing floor at night. This last one was a trifle more scandalous—potentially!

CHAPTER ELEVEN

1. What do you desire more than anything else? It's probably easiest to say that you long for closer fellowship with the LORD or something that sounds suitably "spiritual," but track your thoughts as they wander. Where do they linger? What might that tell you?

2. The next question follows from the example of Hannah. Would you be ready to give whatever that longing is back to the LORD? Further, is it something God would want from you, or is there some preliminary readjustment of desires that might be in order here? What is holding you back from relinquishing control over that deep desire?

3. How have you learned to offer everything (and everyone) to the LORD for his purposes, even those things and people you most treasure? Or is this still a work in progress?

4. It may be the case that you have been misunderstood—perhaps even wrongly accused—by a person or persons in authority. Perhaps even in the church—the modern-day equivalent to Hannah's visit to the Tabernacle. How did you respond? Hannah's declaration that she was praying to God no doubt caused Eli to re-evaluate his rush to judgment. How can we keep our responses measured and God-centered in times of stress?

5. Like Mary's song, Hannah's was brimming with allusions to the words of the Scriptures that were known to her, especially Deut. 32. Spend some time with her song, drawing out the most important themes. How will you bring them into your own life?

CHAPTER TWELVE

1. Do you know anyone who falls into the category of a *naval*? How have you responded to that kind of person? (Classic options are avoidance and vexation.) Pause: What do you think God would have you learn if you were to engage with this person? Use your imagination and ponder how God might, just might be preparing you.

2. Review how Abigail's unpleasant situation was used by God to prepare her for the encounter with David when his anger was about to erupt with dangerous actions. What have you learned from the example of Abigail's faithfulness in the context of what must have felt like a prison for a long time?

3. As you think of Abigail's challenge to David, consider: What did she evidently know, both about him and about the LORD God's purposes, that shaped her response to him? How do her words encourage you?

4. Contemplate the abrupt lifestyle change for Abigail after Nabal's sudden death—leaving wealth, living on the move, and being one of David's "servants" (as she offered to be). Imagine what an equally

radical change might look like in our twenty-first-century environment. Would we be willing to make those changes?

CHAPTER THIRTEEN

1. Sometimes we are in such a hurry to get to Esther's part in her story, we miss the significance of Vashti's bold refusal to obey the king's order to attend his unruly banquet, especially if he was demanding that she attend wearing nothing besides her crown. His drunken demand that she humiliate and display herself led to his being completely humiliated. Have you ever experienced that same kind of reversal from shame to vindication? How did it turn out in the end?

2. Think of all the "strikes" Esther had against her—an orphan, a young woman, and an alien and member of the Jewish minority—and yet God used every part of her identity powerfully. Is this part of your experience, or of people you know? How has God's faithfulness been evident?

3. Mordecai patiently refrained from clamoring for his due recognition for five years. Instead, he let it pass, continued faithfully to watch out for Esther, and maintained his convictions in the face of Haman's public hatred. How do his choices both encourage and challenge you?

4. Describe a situation to which God has brought you that was clearly in the category of "for such a time as this." Was your initial response fear, a sense of inadequacy, or excitement? Did you try get out of it, pray that God would send someone else, resign yourself to the task, or step up? What happened next?

5. The story of Esther is one reversal after another. It's as if God delights in coming out of "hiding" and surprising his people, especially at the last minute! How does this encourage you, especially

the parallel between the apparent absence of God through the entire story and our own seemingly long dry spells?

CHAPTER FOURTEEN AND EPILOGUE

1. Has the Word of God been "lost" for you or those near and dear to you? Why? What roles can the family and the Church play in regaining lost ground?

2. How can we prepare to be like Huldah, able to teach when occasions arise to interpret the Word of God?

3. Think of the fervor of the nationwide revival and Passover celebration so quickly followed by Judah's return to idolatry and the tragic consequences. How could this happen in such a short interval? What parallels do you see between Judah in the sixth century BC and our twenty-first-century western culture? What's different?

4. How can we together work at regaining our deep desire to proclaim the life-restoring truth of the Gospel?

Further Reading

Bailey, Kenneth. *Jesus Through Middle Eastern Eyes: Cultural Studies in the Gospels.* Downers Grove: InterVarsity Press, 2008.

Brownback, Lydia. *Legacy of Faith: From Women of the Bible to Women of Today.* Phillipsburg, NJ: P & R Publishing, 2002.

Fee, Gordon, and Douglas Stuart. *How to Read the Bible for All Its Worth.* Fourth edition. Grand Rapids: Zondervan, 2014.

James, Carolyn Custis. *Lost Women of the Bible: The Women We Thought We Knew.* Grand Rapids: Zondervan, 2005.

Kadlecek, Jo. *Desperate Women of the Bible: Lessons on Passion from the Gospels.* Grand Rapids: Baker, 2006.

Laniak, Timothy A. *While Shepherds Watch Their Flocks: Rediscovering Biblical Leadership.* Shepherd Leader Publications, 2007.

Owens, Virginia Stem. *Daughters of Eve: Women of the Bible Speak to Women of Today.* Colorado Springs: NavPress, 1995.

Phillips, Elaine A. "Esther" in *Expositor's Bible Commentary,* revised edition, vol. 4. Tremper Longman III and David Garland, eds. Grand Rapids: Zondervan, 2010.

Sayers, Dorothy L. *The Man Born to Be King.* San Francisco: Ignatius Press, 1990 (repr).

Contact the author:
elaine.phillips@gordon.edu

Printed in the United States
by Baker & Taylor Publisher Services